T0253070

Making Mu ı ----ɟ

Theory Redux series
Series editor: Laurent de Sutter

Published Titles

Making Multiplicity

Gerald Raunig

polity

First published in 2024 by Polity Press

Polity Press
65 Bridge Street
Cambridge CB2 1UR, UK

Polity Press
111 River Street
Hoboken, NJ 07030, USA

ISBN-13: 978-1-5095-6283-1
ISBN-13: 978-1-5095-6284-8(pb)

A catalogue record for this book is available from the British Library.

Library of Congress Control Number: 2023951577

Typeset in 12.5 on 15pt Adobe Garamond
by Cheshire Typesetting Ltd, Cuddington, Cheshire
Printed and bound by CPI Group (UK) Ltd, Croydon, CR0 4YY

For further information on Polity, visit our website:
politybooks.com

Contents

Introduction

Making multiplicity, fold by fold, folding it further and further. Not just representing, not just claiming, not just praising multiplicity, but making it in struggling for it, in struggles that are themselves manifold. Multiplying the folds, and folding them further and further, staying with multiplicity, machinating multiplicity, making multiplicity in the making.

In the face of intensifying identitarianisms at all levels, from ever new authoritarianisms to attacks on queer and non-binary lifestyles to the fascization and warification of politics and life-worlds, multiplicity must be defended with all our strength. Identitarian, extreme right-wing outgrowths of white supremacism, anti-gender movements, and "great replacement" conspiracy narratives are just the tip of the iceberg: the problem goes much deeper, into the mainstreams of politics, philosophy, and history. At least in the European tradition, there seems to be a meta-historical attraction to the figures and patterns of unity and identity. Since the ancient beginnings of European philosophy, ontological thought has revolved around unity, and that has always meant the one subjugating the many. Reducing the many to the one, leveling the many to the same, sealing the many into one and the same identity – this logic runs through big religions, politics, and philosophies. Again and again, theories of unification and standardization blind out multiplicity and multitude, devaluing them as incomplete, minor, in abeyance and in lack, or subjugating them directly.

In modernity, this domination of unity and identity takes two main forms: on the one hand, extreme individualization, isolation and separation of the individual from their social surround, self-exploitation and self-government; on the other, deindividuation in closing-totalizing, identitarian communities. Today, when capitalism has become machinic, these two poles of the small one and the large One are bundled together in all their contradictions, and they result in a violent whole.

There is no shortage of exemplary figures for this contradictory violence of identity: crazed authoritarian-populist politicians, climate change deniers, Covid deniers, paranoid conspiracy theorists, alliances of Stalinists and libertarians, contrarian thinkers and rage citizens from above and below. For these propagandists of extreme identitarian ideologies, renitence and resilience, refusal and conformity, are closely related. They see themselves as nonconformists and appear as such, while at the same time compliantly serving their scenes, joining into the rage joints – self-pitying trolls and clowns, furiously raging against everything and at the same time adapting on all sides, streamlined to join into the One, continuously passing in the currents of machinic capitalism.

With all their gibberish creation of alternative truths, these querulous contrarians fit in well with the chatbot swarms they babble away to and rampage through, always producing what will potentially gain reach in an ever flexible and adaptable mode. Hateful individuals need hate media, both in the "old" media of TV and giveaway newspapers, as well as in ever new corporate social media. Here, it is not all just junk or garbage or chaotic incoherence, but directed and constantly realigning communication combining identitarian content with algorithmic searches for majorities. Here, floods of disinformation coincide with targeted smear campaigns, here, random spectacles converge with assaults *ad personam*.

At the same time, on a discursive level, practices and philosophies of multiplicity have often been slashed in the recurring figure of "postmodernism." Radical critiques of the state and of capitalism, which analyze and complicate the latter in a timely way as molecular, machinic, and manifold, are thereby attacked as "postmodernist," and with this cheap rhetorical trick are held responsible for precisely these capitalist transformations themselves. Affected by this sleight of hand are all sorts of twentieth-century French philosophers, who may regularly spin in their graves when they hear themselves yet again denigrated as postmodern, anti-political, or anti-social. Most of them made no use of the term postmodernism, and if they did, it was in offensive demarcation from it. Only because they addressed the complex amalgams of European universalism, colonial violence, belief in progress, and capitalist ir/rationality – and because they doubted transcendent models of revolution, opposing them precisely with theories and practices of revolutionary multiplicity – are they attacked under the slogan of postmodernism as nihilistic, culturalist and relativist.

Thus, multiplicity must be defended in its full complexity, in storms and struggles against identitarian domination, unification, and normalization; but it must also (and this is what is at stake in this book) continuously be thought and made: realizing the multiplicity that is there, letting it be when and where it already is, affirming it, preserving and caring for its lines, and at the same time being drawn by these lines, tracing them, drawing them, thus making multiplicity. For this, we need rousing social machines, social movements that queer querulance, that lead contrarian thinking and rage citizenry into the open, disobedience back into the multiplicity from which it comes. For only from multiplicity can multiplicity be made.

What does this mean for a philosophy of multiplicity, for thinking and reading and writing multiplicity, for a text machine that wants to make multiplicity?

First of all, it means that this text machine cannot simply be confused with chatbots, artificial intelligence, and neural networks. Rather, it is a machine precisely insofar as it sets into motion manifold flows between things, living beings, and apparatuses in the production of the text. Not simply the technical apparatus of a typewriter or an AI language model, but the multiplicity of desiring-production and the sociality of a writing process that goes beyond writing in the narrow sense. Writing flows out of and into thinking and reading, overflowing its banks and the never quite clear boundaries of activity and passion. The text machine stretches across apparatuses, gadgets, things, materials, bodies, and spirits, flowing between and around them, appending and connecting to both minor pasts and novel readings.

In relation to the assemblages of thinking, reading, and writing, multiplicity means precisely not writing about multiplicity, but writing multiplicity, making it, and still doing so in reading and thinking. Multiplicity in the making of the text is a constant experimentation with the forms of the text, with its forms of organization, its modes of enunciation, its assemblages of publication – against the striations of scholarly writing in the academic publication apparatus, which with all its standardizations and hierarchizations becomes its own gravedigger; against an aggressively anti-scientific style that serves its bubbles in an errant, short-winded, and querulous manner; but also against an analytical, know-it-all style of classic authoritarian criticism that serves, analogously to institutional forms of organization, to establish and confirm state apparatuses. Instead of building parallel apparatuses of individual-authoritarian writing and ordering-political organizing, we need to conjoin the text machines with the social machines. The revolutionary multiplicity of the text machines emerges in modes of enunciation, usages, and instituent practices that do not conceive micro-socialities, social struggles, and social movements as outside, nor the text as an instrument for their analysis or for strategic prescription and instruction. Connecting and appending, producing proximities even at a distance, text conjoins with social struggle.

Dividuum (Semiotext(e)/MIT, 2016) and *Dissemblage* (Minor Compositions, 2022) are a two-volume attempt to approach the dividuality and unruly multiplicity of social machines and text machines from different historical-political perspectives and in different forms of writing, with multiple materials and twenty-two socio-poetic ritornellos. The present text aims to use the framework of Theory Redux to intensify these approaches, condensing the central contents of those two books into seventeen concepts, without necessarily reducing the machinic-machinating capacity of theory and text.

These seventeen conceptual machinations are by no means finely delineated units, their outlines neatly drawn and separated from one another, but rather overlapping, interlocking, mutually approximating components of a fraying and unruly conceptual assemblage. Components, composing levers, wheels, and edges of a composition that care for their surrounds, conceptual surrounds that in turn oscillate and resonate and machinate with the surrounds of social machines and their technical as well as political compositions. Not so much individual concepts, but rather mutual machinations, concepts like machine and multiplicity resist identification and determination; they rather machinate and multiply themselves and their assemblages.

And with all this making and machinating of multiplicity, there will still never have been the one maker, the one machinator and his material, because it is the materials that work, the socialities that think, the things that write, the machines that machinate. Always there will have been several, a multiplicity of makers and things to be made, rampant middles without head or captain. And they dance the transversal intellect: multilingual reading circles, long-term laptops and five-year smartphones, bars as part-time offices, inviting editors, unruly doors, secret central secretaries and sub-concierges, double-sided printouts, careless notes, brief interruptions of runs and of dreams to capture sudden streams of ideas rather unsuccessfully on pieces of paper, sound sessions and riso experiments, paperbacks and garden desks, philosophical specters in their graves and elsewhere, living ghostly voices and more or less animate things that belong to no one, centennial, a century old or more, subsistential terrains and whole barrios, deckchairs in the floodplain, last reader and first reader, and the many from Ritornello 1 and Ritornello 22, desiring the return and becoming of condividual multiplicity.

I

Of Machinic Capitalism

Capital has long been a machine, insofar as it flows
and overflows, joins and appends, establishes
connections everywhere. Since the bourgeois
revolutions, all that is solid melts into air, and
meanwhile the machinations and mutations of
the machine maintain and promote a versatile
traffic. As unconfined and open as possible, connecting and appending, ubiquitously. In the end,
this is also what constitutes the machine at its
core: it is not a mere instrument, not a tool,
not an extension nor an expansion of the human
body. It is not simply a technical apparatus in
the service of man. It is an assemblage, a social
machine, a desiring machine; it can ultimately
also become a revolutionary machine, and with

it, between gaseousness and solid matter, there are constant flows in many directions, flows of data, flows of becoming, not least flows of sociality and desire.

When I pick up my smartphone, I'm not just picking up a tool like a hammer or a cleaning sponge, isolated and instrumental. When I stroke its surface, I'm not just stroking the smooth coating of a technical device. I am stroking a virtual sociality, I am stroking it and bracing myself with it. It is the machinic flows between technical apparatuses, social assemblages, living bodies, and techno-things that enable multiple intercourse. Following the machinic flows of desire, social virtuality and social reality sometimes merge, and I become part of the machinic flow. But being appended to the machines can also lead to dependence, to material and affective dependence on the permanency of the flows, on the continuity of the connection, on the incessancy of the data streams.

At the same time, the workers were never mere accessories of the technical apparatuses, appendages limited to the simplest manual operations on them. There has always been a transversal intellect at work, which started and kept running the manifold joinings and interlockings of technical and social machines. Working on the machines, workers have always invented, operated, and revolutionized this stream of intellect, affect, and matter to the same extent as they perform their daily and hourly service on the machines.

The machinic accompanies capitalism as a component of liquefaction and deformation, and at the same time joining and connection, but it currently also takes on new forms. The term "machinic capitalism" therefore makes double sense: the machine in its continuous flowing out and connecting is a fundamental conceptual component of capitalism, but it also mutates anew – through the economic and ecological transformations of the last five decades – stuttering, collapsing, and continuously crisis-ridden, and yet ceaselessly paving its way.

But the common narratives and interpretations of these transformations often miss the point. On the surface, the new meaning of the machinic in capitalism is identified with the proliferation of technological devices: the threat of takeovers by artificial superintelligence, the invasions of smart technologies into the private sphere and of mechanical prostheses into the body. All these developments are real, but the machinic goes beyond them. It takes on its current meaning primarily as the insatiable appetite of machinic capitalism for ever new data to traverse, as the flows of desire for being online and appended to technical gadgets, for being disposable, enjoined and disposed, for joining, joint next to joint.

Disposability is the central component of machinic capitalism. The universal coloniality inherent in the latter requires an ever new advance into areas not yet thoroughly capitalized and their colonization. Again and again, the accumulation that stood at its origin must return and find new objects of appropriation and cooptation. Colonization of the commons; colonization of the relation of workers to their subsistential territories and their means of production; colonization of social reproduction; colonization in the proper sense of the violent seizure of land by settlers – with the tendency to colonize all continents, to develop all seas, to appropriate the whole globe, soon also space, finally looping and spiraling through not only new, undiscovered territories, but all possible reserves, which are to be accumulated anew and in new ways.

In this process, the colonial figure of the blank space on the map as a *tabula rasa* is repeated in all possible forms. Again and again, subsistential territories, lives, and habitats are erased. Scraped maps, overwritten rather than blank sheets, slates of colonial appropriation. Still there is exploitation of mineral resources and labor assets, but also new forms of enslavement: social reproduction and affective labor are overcoded, subsistential territories taken into service, the transversal intellect enclosed and appropriated as intellectual property.

Beyond the disposability of goods and labor power, machinic capitalism is increasingly fueled by the machinic accumulation of data. The continuous process of expropriation now tends more than ever towards the arbitrary: randomly accumulating data only to be able to traverse it. Sometimes this does not even require enclosure or appropriation, but just certain forms of use. Regardless use, disinterested use, use without care, unsuspended and incessant use, limitless use, use that is ruthlessly interested in more and more data to which it has not yet had access: ceaseless search movements that want to mine new data, in a mine that is a perfect immanence field, a no longer containable whole, but fraying immanence. While classical processes of accumulation were primarily processes of identification, enclosure, and expropriation, in machinic capitalism these processes no longer seem to be entirely necessary, superseded by mechanisms of open, endless, and for the time being purposeless accumulation and traversal in all directions.

Artificial intelligence has little interest in the individual data, in the individuals whose data it feeds on, whether they write utility texts or world literature, whether they simply surf the net or conduct targeted queries, whether they seek partnerships or information, whether they control drones or smart envelopments. As long as intelligence agencies or insurance companies are not interested in them, the digital footprints and virtual profiles of the individuals are irrelevant, too. On the other side, artificial intelligences have all the more appetite for the amount of dividually traversable data they can assemble. It is a gathering, not a devouring, even if the hunger is insatiable. There is no digestion going on, just the assembly and preserving of data sets, which enable infinite traversals as an eternal and eternally expanding archive.

Accumulation in machinic capitalism operates in a threefold manner: Firstly, there are search movements in all directions, spreading, distributing, scattering over many places. Stretching out as far as they can, encompassing as much as possible, dividual lines extend into the remotest areas. In apparent contrast, the second component is that of accumulation, of bundling, of making clusters disposable. But it is precisely this combination of dispersion and bundling which, in machinic capitalism, is the prerequisite for, thirdly, traversing the bundles dividually.

It is not individuals and their cooperations that are at the center of contemporary modes of production but, more and more, the dividual lines that traverse individuals. Dividuality implies dividedness, but in relation neither to individual parts nor to an imagined whole of their community; not the separateness of the whole of individual things, but their scattering, which extends through various individual things. The dividual emerges in the drawing of dividual lines, which traverse and bundle the subsistings. Scattered through different individuals, the separate components of the dividual gather on dividual lines.

This property of assembling along dividual lines is not unique to machinic-capitalist accumulation, but it is in this sphere that we find some central applications of the principle of dispersion, bundling, and dividual traversal. The financial instrument of the derivative derives from the value of the future composition of commodities, as speculation on their possible future value, as trading in risks, as betting on those risks. Often widely dispersed commodities are divided here, and these parts of commodities are bundled with the parts of other commodities. Through this recomposition and risk calculation, the dividual derivative becomes worth more than the individual commodities. While the individual wholes remain in their places – whether a gold deposit, an apartment in a ghost-*urbanización* completed only for this purpose, or the future value of an education – the traffic of derivatives goes in all directions spatially and temporally, speculating on their parts and their accumulations and compositions in all possible magnitudes in an abstract way. Here, too, the interest in individuals is kept within limits; what is relevant is dividuality, masses, and their recomposition and mobility. This dividual logic of derivatives no longer manifests itself only in economic flowcharts, calculations, and predictions – in representations of the future that entail management actions. The role of technological components such as algorithms and mathematical models is no longer simply to calculate risks so that management can control and minimize those risks. The algorithms play with ever greater risks; indeed they virtually produce them, thus extending the colonizing function of dividual-machinic capitalism.

The situation is similar in the field of data mining: the accumulation and assembly of data in order to make it disposable and traversable on a dividual basis. This is not simply data collection in the traditional sense of the collection and ordering of individual data sets by authorities, intelligence agencies, banks or insurance companies. Through the development of machine readability, the processing and searchability of data, the disposability and traversability of the now dividual data, becomes central. The resulting huge data banks do not work towards a final totalization of the data, but rather towards its incomplete and perpetual expansion and ultra-colonial enclosure and extraction.

In the face of fascization, techno-government and neo-authoritarianism, ecological crisis and climate catastrophe, political repression and new racisms, nationalist cleavages and new wars and civil wars, it is not simply that the bourgeois classes once again conspire against the proletariat in a compliant pact with authoritarianisms and the extreme right. It is not simply that the lumpenproletariats are turning into fascist baiting masses, complacent, submissive, and subservient. And it is not simply that the lack of organization of the working classes prevents technical composition from turning into political composition.

Rather, it is our techno-social modes of behavior, forms of production, and struggles that are changing, and, with them and through them, it is capitalism itself that is transforming into a now dividual machinic capitalism. This transformation occurs not only at the so-called macro level, but above all in those aspects that permeate all scales, the mutating forms of use, conduct, and life that in and through machinic capitalism increasingly take the form of anti-sociality.

Daily and hourly we perform our service at the machines, no longer only nine-to-five at the assembly line, but continuously on the line of an online life, pulled on and pulled up by the line, taken into service by it, subservient to it, constantly disposable to the line. In the mode of modulation, there is movement on all sides, drawing a line, being drawn by it, ceaselessly improving it and improving ourselves. This is machinic subservience: not only servitude, subjugation, enslavement to machinery, but also at the same time self-government: a perpetual optimization of machinic selves and machines. Life on the line is life on the leash, and this leash is short.

Not only online work, but also private communications via corporate social media, doctor's appointments, travel bookings, cab rides, pizza orders, bank transfers, weather reports, ticket purchases, and dealings with the authorities are all handled via this short leash. And on this same short leash, completely new, conformist and comfortable modes of conduct emerge. In the continuous fit of conforming assemblages, subjugation is paired with self-government. Work and life finally become indistinguishable: in home offices, old and new forms of the appropriation of labor merge smoothly with the colonization of private territories.

Appending and depending on the machines increases the risk of psychopathological problems, attention deficits, anxiety, narcissism, and rage disorders, not only as the attrition of online existence, but also as addictive behavior in the networks of corporate social media. With pandemics, war, and the increase of all possible forms of violence, the renitent-resilient dispositions of the "rage citizen" thrive in the midst of these compliant, conformist, comfortable behaviors, as a paradoxical complex of renitence and subservience less to a sovereign than to (self-)compliance in the joints of rage.

Meanwhile, imagination in matters of the future, especially in the booming fields of AI and machine learning, is extremely poor: what a ridiculous lack of imagination is apparent when today's pseudo-philosophical spokesmen of corporate social media and artificial intelligence lag far behind a novel of 1968 imagining the year 1992, for example, with regard to the questions of whether organic androids dream of electric sheep, whether they have a soul, whether they can be lonely, or whether the technical examination of their eye muscles can and should enable them to be distinguished from humans.

The algorithms of artificial intelligence, meanwhile, are always on the hunt for what lies outside their territory and its im/probabilities. In this greedy search for new colonies, they are virtually defined by what they are not yet and what they may never become. And with them chase the traders and longtermists as individual-human protagonists of dividual-machinic capitalism, however unimaginative their inventions and visions of the future. Their machination is the not-knowing of the future that has become a market of predictions and preventions, of pretension and delusion. Their fantasies are pervaded by the image of the *tabula rasa* beyond presupposition and past. Their present is a blank slate.

2

Of Dividuality and Condivision

It is only because the primacy of the individual is such an unquestioned part of our conception of existence, with all its aspects of right, territory, property, and anti-sociality, that we give little thought to the problematic construction of the undividedness and indivisibility of the modern individual in particular. The individual is a whole, a one, and arranges all its properties into this wholeness and unity. It is dissimilar and sovereign, and it is individual through the fullness and completion of its substantial and accidental properties, a fullness that shares nothing, not even the multiplicity from which it comes.

Before the in-dividual, however, there must obviously have been something that called up its linguistic negative: *dividuum*, the dividual, dividuality. But negativity and opposition are figures far too simplistic to express the dividual. If a relation can be described here at all, then dividuality as multiplicity crosses a double unity: the indivisible-one of isolated-separated individuality and the all-one of closing-totalizing community.

It is both these poles of oneness and unity – individuality and community – that dividuality breaks through: Individuality with its characteristics of separation and dissimilarity; individuality that sets itself up as sovereign and separate. Community as wholeness and substance, union and totality, *com-munitas*, *con* and *munus*; community with its derivatives persisting in the logic of totalization and communion or the subtraction of the *munus* that must be paid as a levy for participation in the community.

For the classical doctrines of modern capitalism, possessive individualism was the central driving force. In opposition to this, deindividuation was understood as the greatest danger, threatening not just dehumanization, but above all a separation of the self from its possession: becoming possessed was at stake, both as the always implicit possibility of losing self-ownership in serfdom and enslavement, but also that of the non-normalized, the deviant, the loony possessed. Both entailed exclusion from personhood. But in the more and more dividual economy of machinic capitalism, a decoupling and recoupling of human possession and dehumanizing, reifying deindividuation is taking place. This once dialectical relationship is replaced by a contradictory complementarity of possessive individualism and deindividuation: while individual possession is obsessively marked and exercised, capitalist value creation at the same time shows itself less and less interested in individuals, whether human individuals or thing-individuals. Even if every individual has its chip implanted, wears its electronic collar, and carries its navigation app, what needs to be tracked, valorized, and controlled are the mobilities and relationships of masses, tracking not only each person's position but their relations of proximity. In smart cities, wooden skyscrapers, vertical forests, and heated sidewalks meet cameras, microphones, wireless networks, and sensor systems. The sidewalks are not only heated, they are also equipped with pressure sensors to measure movement. The vertical gardens measure not only the humidity of the air, but also the temperature of their inmates. The wooden walls ensure the unhindered flow of radio and wireless signals. Conformingly, the masses produce and deliver data. Deprived of all subsistence, the territory becomes a deterritorialized reserve, a colony of modulation, a disposable city. Here, possessive individualism and deindividuation form a violent whole that drives the mechanisms of dispersion, accumulation, and dividual traversal.

But this is only one side of dividuality. The dividual can also actualize its quality of dispersion differently than as the spread of algorithmic-derivative dividuality with which we live in machinic capitalism. It can be understood as a new, manifold form of gathering and bracing on dividual lines, an assembly that no longer consists only in the meeting and joining of individuals; an assembly not on a straight, aligning line of adjustment, but in ruptures, leaps, unjoined; an assembly on dividual lines, a gathering that gathers and assembles with the gathered at the same time.

This form of gathering in dispersion, of sharing in division, of bracing in farnearness, is as novel as it is recurrent, and it virtually also calls for new forms of economy and ecology, and of law.

Colonial genealogies inscribe law in a gridded and gridding logic, the logic of property and the primacy of the individual. Among the preconditions of Eurocentric juridical discourses is the instance of a responsible and indivisible individual, a legal person who, by virtue of being identifiable, can also assume undivided responsibility. Law and property are bound to this individual subject on the one hand, and to a precisely defined and identified territory on the other. Against this legal conglomerate of individual, territory, and property, it is possible to think of constitutions that build not on the individual and its property, but on dividual usages beyond property and individualization; of concepts of territoriality that do not build on land ownership and the rigid cadastralization even of the past of property, but place a dividual ecology of subsistential territories in the foreground of law.

Such an understanding of law can break the violent context of possessive individualism and deindividuation without paving the way for domineering processes of disenfranchisement, the introduction of lawless states, or the governmental informalization of law. Dividual law can overcome the Eurocentric realm of law on its own terrain. Tendentially, traces of dividual law can be found in expansions of the notion of the individual even in classical law – for example, in the construction of firms, associations, and other "personhoods" along the lines of individuals as legal persons, and more so in indigenous notions of law based on the vague idea that other entities such as animals, trees, the deceased, deities, and the earth as a whole can have rights. But as important as it is to decolonize the Euroanthropocentric aspects of law, the insistent power of the individual even in non-"Western" cosmologies should not be overlooked. To disrupt the classical law of individual, territory, and property, analogies to the individual will not suffice; more radically still, we must assume queer machinic dividualities that evoke resonances and approximations, that joint and brace multiplicity. With this primacy of dividual law quite different usages can be generated, before and beyond the identification of individuals or the structural analogy to individual law.

Usages – that is, what in poststructural theory are somewhat awkwardly also called modes of subjectivation. Usages are forms of use, sometimes even in the absence of a particular object of this use, as objectless and non-objectifying customs, as modes of conduct, *usages de vie*, whole ways of life, or modes of existence. While usages in machinic capitalism increasingly take an anti-social form, dividuality also shimmers as a faculty of co-formity and bracing. Dividual usages are divisible and connectable, never quite alone and never whole, always before wholeness, before the indivisibility of the individual, in manifold exchange with other ways of life and thing-worlds. Whereas indivisibility implies the negation of sharing, divided and sharing dividuality joins the parts and at the same time allows them to be out of joint, rather than unifying and uniting them. Here, the dividual is not only linguistically prior to any individuality, it points to the primacy of jointing and bracing in multiplicity. Dividual multiplicity, dividual division and condividual sharing are before individuality and surround it, traverse it, as a fraying and sprawling spread, a multiplicity of situated machines.

In such a perspective, even the labored and detouring conceptualization of transindividuality becomes obsolete, because dividuality does not need the subsequent interconnection of individuality through the prefix trans, but is before any individuality, joined and unruly, before individuals are constituted that would grow beyond their individuality and become transindividual.

So, if we start from the primacy of dividuality, in all its ambivalence, we can also say: Yes, the leash of online life is short, but this leash is pulled from more than one side. Not only do desires of machinic subservience appear in being kept on the leash, in being attracted to the line, but dividual production of desire also runs over the same lines. Revolutionary lines pull on this leash, and perhaps the leash even breaks, in a *Nu*, in an instant, when the desiring machines overflow and collapse.

As an unruly joining, dividuality becomes a factor of new forms of organizing and social convergence. Here it is the dispersed virtual composition of a multiplicity of situated practices whose expansion does not function classically through the mediation of parties and media or as a process of international solidarity alone, but as a transversal machine that appears in many places at once and as their bracing, at the same time, with situated practices and social movements themselves. On dividual lines, a gathering and bundling occurs that does not take the form of unification, but one of a manifold bracing at a distance. This bracing attribute of dividuality is not limited to an abstract and normative figure; it has recurred in recent decades as a dividual joining and farnear bracing of struggles, as a practice in the social movements, where local struggles develop more or less simultaneously in different places and from the beginning in an intertwined and mutually influential way, without origin, without linear development and without unification. This happened with the occupation movements in Mediterranean countries, which spread over large parts of the world as Occupy, as well as in the municipalist movements of the 2010s, in the Latin American feminist strike, and in the worldwide ecological struggles of the 2020s.

Dividual usages bring forth new forms of conduct, whole forms of life, ways of living together, convivialities, but also new forms of composition. The dividual points to a collectivity beyond unity, purity, and wholeness, a collectivity that is also not in simple opposition to the individual. While even communism and the commons carry the problem of *communitas*, in the sense of potentially totalizing closure, as a conceptual burden, in the composition of multiplicity in theory and practice it is necessary to consider both division and sharing, dividuality and joining, separation and co-formity, which in a theory of the dividual can be conceptualized as condividuality and condivision.

Condivisione is Italian for "sharing something with each other," and it is found only in that language: the Italian *condividere* is *compartir* in Spanish, *partager* in French, *teilen* in German, *to share* in English, but *condivisione* linguistically resists the communal and totalizing connotations of sharing as well as the divisive-negative logic of *munus* and *com-munitas*, according to which one must contribute in order to participate, to belong, to be part of the community. This resistance to both the subtractive and totalizing logics of community is not just a linguistic issue, but a deeply political one. In contrast to the communitarian perspective of *communitas*, condivision contains and processes both division, separation, disjunction, dissociation, and *con-*, sharing, joining, conjunction, association – gathering in a non-communitarian, non-unifying, non-reductive mode of composition. In the sharing of being divided, as unruly bond and dispersed bracing, condivision names and operates, thinks and makes, the political composition of multiplicity.

3

Of the Middle

Unwillingly and defiantly, condividual revolution shares one and the same field of immanence with machinic capitalism. Yet it is precisely in this ambiguous terrain that lines can be drawn, dividual lines, queer lines, revolutionary lines that do not lead to a phantasmatic absolute outside of capitalism, but on their way discover anti-capitalist, revolutionary praxis. Drawing lines, being drawn by them, continuing to draw lines, and being drawn by them, finding other lines, and being found by them: anti-capitalist praxis develops on the same terrain, in the same middle, on the same field of immanence.

This philosophy of immanence is deeply materialistic, and the immanent middle is a middle of matters and power relations. Never is the middle empty, a neutral vessel, a mere container or empty center. It is not an empty land that can be occupied without circumstance, as if there were nobody there, nobody's land. In it, all forms of relation take place, including violence, domination, and power relations. Asymmetries spread and mutate, domineering hierarchizations as well as manifold empowerments.

The middle is the field of immanence, and it has no outside, no beyond, no transcendence. It is the fraying, sprawling, mutating, immanence field of machinic capitalism and condividual revolution. It is without beginning and end, without clear separation, transversal to oppositionality, dialectics, mediation, and sublation. Milieu of milieus, it is a medium, but not as a channel or mediation towards another world; passive-active, mediopassive, the middle extends in all directions.

Never is the middle a static and clearly delineated, regulated and disciplined land. It is fraying, and it is never whole. It is not a mainstream, enjoined into mediocrity, but a middle that may lose its horizon and fail to hold its banks, an immanence that is ready to overflow on all sides.

If the middle cannot be confined to a particular center, it remains *mi-lieu*, French for a place in the middle, rather than a milieu in the sense of the environment around something, enveloping something else, enclosing it, as a condition to which those inside would be exposed, as social or spatial structuring, an outside to a subject at the inner center.

Multiplicity is neither an antecedent nor a future whole; it populates the middle on which dividual lines can be drawn and exert attraction. Drawing the lines never erases multiplicity but divides it, consolidates it and recomposes an immanence field. Making multiplicity is medial: drawing lines and being drawn by them, lines that can only be drawn in the doing. To draw dividual lines in the middle and through the middle, and to be drawn by them, is as simultaneously active and passive as the grammatical form of the medium, the mediopassive, the middle voice in some Indo-European languages – when a subject is active and at the same time affected by the action, when the subject becomes object at the same time: letting oneself be drawn by the line, coming into the flow, getting into the middle. To make multiplicity means to let oneself fall into the middle, making not in a masculinist but in a queer-mystical-mediopassive way. And if the middle is never empty, then no *creatio ex nihilo* can be thought, but only the middle as stream and ecology, in which the dichotomies of subject and object, author and audience, active and passive lapse in favor of a letting and letting go, a caring company with all of what is there.

With this shared terrain in the middle, there is yet no confusion, and certainly no compliance, between capitalism and revolution. A free market is not liberation. Artificial general intelligence is not transversal intellect. Diversity is not multiplicity. There is no simple affirmation and acceleration of capitalism, pushing it over some phantasmal cliff, as with the accelerationists or transhumanists or extropianists. Nor is there any dialectic that can be revolutionarily sublated; there are only and precisely the lines, the resistances, the struggles of condividual revolution.

The lines of condividual revolution are primary. From the capitalist point of view, they are pre-drawn lines that can be traced, more or less without circumstance, in valorization, takeover, appropriation. What one gets is taken, what falls into one's hands is exploited. But the lines are also precisely the lines that make capitalism and its forms of exploitation and subjugation leak and lose control, lines that not only lead to revolution, but are revolutionary themselves.

The temporality of the middle is not a present as a point between past and future; it is the dilatated present time beyond utopia, beyond obsessions with the future. In dilatated present time, the revolutionary line can be drawn without the logic of prefiguration, without the enclosed prospect of a future society, without the tunnel vision of the grand plan. And there is also no tipping point, like the techno-utopian "singularity" or the one-dimensionally interpreted ecological catastrophe, but only the all-around possible mutation of the immanence field by the weight and speed of the many lines.

The dividual lines that draw us, attract us, and pull us through are never straight lines; they wend, windy and winding, drawing their courses and breaking out of them in incisions, ruptures, rebellious presences. They expand the immanence field, driving it and shifting its boundaries. We lie in wait, lurking, for the return of upheaval, overthrow, soft riot, *Nu*. Then the fraying, flowing middle becomes a rampant middle, a middle in which things pick up speed or start to swirl, a middle that carries things along, a passive-active milieu of mutation, the rampant middle of con-dividual revolution.

4

Of Assembly, Farnearness, and Becoming Similar

In some poststructural theories there is a lasting and comprehensible resentment against similarity. Such theories have repeatedly thematized similarity as an instrument for leveling. Its bad reputation stems from its role in processes of adaptation, in which it appears as nothing more than a difference pressed into templates, unified, and already on its way to becoming identity. In perceiving individuals and individual things and determining their similarities in comparison, an alignment takes place. The blending of similarity and oneness, resembling and unifying, already shows up in the changing connotations of the Latin *similis* and its relatives after the Indo-European root **sem-* for "one."

Similarity can indeed also be a social component of as-similation as alignment, as the many being reduced to one, as adaptation to the normalized, as integration into the standard measure. Clearly and distinctly problematized in contemporary anti-racist discourses, assimilation as well as integration are tools used by dominant discourses to construct their outside. On the one hand, the construction of this outside produces political exclusion effects through increasingly extreme border regimes, a necropolitics of the border, and mobilization against all forms of freedom of movement. On the other hand, it serves to exploit and incorporate the autonomy of migration, integrating the outside into the inside, into the pure, the whole, the normal, the same – according to a rule of assimilation, without granting anything even close to equal rights. Instead of preserving similarity as a process, its adaptation in the reactionary game of identity and absolute difference leads towards old and new racisms, which appear also in the guise of culturalism and identitarianism.

With the enjoining mechanisms of machinic capitalism, similarity can be put to even more complex use as a precondition for processing multiplicity. In these machinic procedures, assimilation as approximation is a modulating process that qualitatively modulates what is innumerably manifold, immeasurable, not to be modularized, not quantitatively gradable. Machinic search movements bring things, people, and their parts into order according to similarities. Here, similarity is transformed from a possible interface of social intercourse into a modulating principle of order, pressing polyphony into a comparable tonality, as resonances of the similar become sliding consonances, enjoining unisons.

In online advertising, this gives rise to processes of adaptation that handle similarities without necessarily having to generate units or measure them. On the one hand, creating and tracking user profiles with individual timelines, expressions of interest, and likes form the basis for advertising that is no longer simply target-group oriented but completely personalized. On the other hand, this involves traversing other data sets and searching for comparable data, leading to invocations such as "users like you like items like this." Similarity ("like you," "like this") here also seems to have affective quality ("to like"). It is the fit that pleases, a modern version of "like will attract like." The like corresponds to a manifestation of liking, but instead of affection, the most important function is the pressing of the like button, which leaves a digital trace in the user profile, which in turn enables processes of comparison and assimilation in the big data traffic.

In addition to the sales effect created by the assumed similarity of affect, here it is apparently mainly approximation, the convergence of the desires of different individuals, which is focused on and valorized as far as possible. But there is also the seemingly opposite case, in which approximation is to be prevented and the tracking of data is to serve primarily to maintain distances. Nevertheless, this is still about proximity: when the ambiguous term "social distancing" emerged as a result of the Covid-19 pandemic, it was unclear whether an ethical practice of physical distance or an anti-social conduct in control society was to be tested here. In any case, the traffic of Covid suspects was to be tracked, either by identifying individual location or by dividual data doubles. Lengthy discussion of the different Covid apps culminated in two different ways of tracking. On the one hand, location data was about identifying individuals at specific places; on the other hand, proximity data was about their changing proximities. Dividual logic prevailed here as well, in the relational determination of proximities instead of individual position and identification: the production of distances and directed proximities can best be accomplished dividually, relationally, and en masse. In this way, self-government becomes machinically subservient and valorized, but so does the relationship between self-governing subjects. Instead of the logic of measurement, identification, and control, proximities, probabilities, and similarities are modulated and mobilized.

But what if similarity resists alignment and enjoining in measurement and modulation? What if it is precisely the way to subvert the one and the comparison, both in its form of identity (which is absolute difference) and in the process of modulation? What if, on the contrary, it is bent on a tide of ungovernable bracing and spreading that never quite subsides, remaining vague and not quite edged? What if similarity is precisely that which allows the distant to come close, to approach, yet in doing so never tunes it, never aligns it, but leaves it out of tune, out of disposal, out of control?

This turn of similarity from the compulsion to conform into something that cannot be conformed is of enormous importance today. All of today's struggles take the form of a struggle for this mode of similarity, for a similarity that does not serve to deliver the measured, like the non-measurable, to the machinic order but provides for a bracing of the farnear. To draw again on the Indo-European root *sem- for "one" and the genealogy of the Latin *similitudo*: the Romance words for similarity and the term assimilation derive from this root, but also the German word Ver*samm*lung and the English as*sem*bly and as*sem*blage.

When resemblance and similarity are conceptualized as forms and processes of mutual becoming they become components of assembling. Similarity that crosses the dichotomy of identity and difference is not a static state that can be identified, but a becoming similar that constitutes dividuality as divisible sharing, as middle and joint, thus also its potentiality of connecting and appending, of bracing and joining, of assembly, of co-formity.

Co-formity is the decisive component of assembling in becoming similar. Not at all uniform, co-formity keeps the forms becoming similar. With it, the assembly remains unruly and disposable, incapable of being captured in a leveling whole. Similarity remains nonsensual-nonsensical, neither sensually nor systematically graspable in a direct way. Such an unruly form of similarity cannot simply be sensually or rationally ascertained; neither perceived nor understood as established similarity, it can only be generated; not as a being similar that can be stated of two objects in comparison, but as a processual becoming similar that takes place in and as the co-formity of mutating forms.

Similarity is not antecedent in certain individual things. It does not proceed from the presupposition of an individual thing which, on the basis of this presupposition, would differ from a given other individual thing and then become similar to this other thing. Becoming similar is a capacity that arises precisely not in perceptual comparison but in exchange. The components of this exchange are rarely only human beings, but include the multiple mutual resemblance of things, machines, and living beings, more or less animate. What constitutes becoming similar is the co-formity in space and sociality, but also in time. For kin who are lurking for the return of kin from long ago, becoming similar is goalless and endless approximation, transmutation, multiple and mutual relation, however asymmetrical it may be, resemblance, far distant and next door.

Quite counter to the intuition of the similarity of proximity, as in consanguinity or the proximity of grasses in a meadow, becoming similar does not mean putting together or thinking together the nearest and closest in each case, but rather the constellation of near and far, farnearness. The image of the smart family at the dinner table, children and parents equally engrossed in their smartphones, may be a dystopian figure of the addictive potential of appending to the machines, but the constellation of farnearness means something quite different. There is another potential in the practice of appending to the machines, when new technologies and gadgets bring distant desires closer together, creating proximities in the distance, new farnear rhythms and ritornellos. And perhaps farnearness itself is still relevant at the same dinner table, as the potentiality of escape from familialism and the proximity forced by being born into it.

Farnearness is a distance that arises at the same time as the proximities it braces. With it a similarity asserts itself which insists on its dissimilarity, which keeps at a distance and keeps the distance, however small it may be. If it is co-forming, it lets the many forms subsist; if it corresponds, then it does so only in an odd way; if it gathers, then it gathers the dissimilar next to each other or scatters neighbors to different places. As assembly, becoming similar can be a contraction and condensation of distant positions, or their relaxation, their extension to the far distant. Farnearness can cause an excess of bracing and unbracing under the sign of multiplicity, attraction, and being attracted, assembling as dissemblage; an unruly joining not only of people, but as an approximation of the distant in the approach of living bodies and technical apparatuses, in appending to the machines, in machinic subjoinings: haptic, auditory, visual, not simply dystopic or euphoric, but testing the possibilities of an infinitive becoming similar.

5

Of Minor Voices and Windy Kin

When a grand voice resounds, from far above and a long way away, not only do the many minor voices fall silent. With their silencing, the capacity of gathering also seems to wane. Not that they want to hear this grand voice so much, this undisturbed and amplified voice, protected by consanguinity and filiation from father to son. But the form of their assembly, their many-voiced choir, is in this way hierarchized and structuralized and orchestrated, so that the assembly gathers them as individuals, units, and unity. The one grand voice drowns out everything, leaving the cacophonous multiplicity down here behind.

Will the minor voices listen away, or cover their ears? Will they evade the show?

Who knows, but as always they will also prick up their ears and try to listen to the small sounds, the background noises and the overtones, very close and further away, listen to the thing-world and the spirit-world with all their noise and all their racket, listen to voices with machinic ears, listen to the air, to the wind and around corners. Echoes from lives gone by, half-loud voices from untracked geographies, a sudden sound like a word, a rumble, a creak not forgotten forever. Harking and humming, the minor voices pave their dividual lines through echoing times and pulsating space.

A minor voice eludes the majority that is inflicted upon it. It is minor in the sense that it does not simply fit into the counting logic of majority and minority. It is disposable only to its swarm of voices. The minor voice is not a diminished, not a reduced voice. It drifts in the noise of a subjuncture, of which it is a part, and in the songs of the things around. Queer voice, squeaky voice, windy falsetto, leaning back in becoming minor, letting itself sink into multiplicity, because only in becoming minor and letting itself fall does the capacity of the dispersed-braced revolution arise, the condividual revolution.

Into the subjuncture the minor voice disjoins, and when it lets go of the self, it also leaves the binary logic of gender. It queers the binary apparatus, dismisses the gender difference, flouts the professional order of male/female gendered voices; as the active/passive middle voice of a rampant queer middle, it defects from the division and the hierarchy of the registers, bass-soprano and alto-falsetto, without much discipline, without hitting the notes, without staying in key.

The voice does not want to drown out anything, it does not want to drone, or to overrule the other voices; it wants to remain minor, in order to be able to become several: dividual voices that sound subjoined under each other, scattered around each other, in search of other voices, convergence and a gathering of the minor voices. The more they become, the more minor they become, striving apart in resonance.

And an unruly wind makes them kindred. Their voice kin, bound without blood bonds, needing no DNA comparison, no parental testing. Nor is it an elective affinity, a considered choice of kin, a sovereign decision in free will. Neither blood nor choice connects the minor voices, but soul kinship, which also touches the things, and the machines and the ghosts and the codes. Voice kin, soul-code kin, unexpected souls that expected us after all, kindred ghosts – we are possessed by them, more or less animate things, they belong to no one, *animae*, blowing in the wind, drifty, windy kin.

Like a leaf in the wind, light, too light perhaps, lightweight anyway, too lighthearted to linger. A wind that blows through the joints like the heavenly child, down here and next door: At every door there shall be many joints / That's where the wind comes in. All attempts to sing in unison fail, and the voices retune each other, sway each other, windy kin, windy voices. And sometimes windy kin become resistant kin. Not just simply as the wind blows away the seeds – random dispersal, scattering, contagion – but also as an uprising, revolt, mutiny in an instant, in a *Nu*. Then the storm rises, *levante*, freshening from the east.

Music that seems to come from nowhere, and perhaps it really does come from nowhere, from a very specific nothingness, a manifold, a full and bulging nothingness, because music is already playing before the music starts to play, before and behind the stage. Before the show, before the spectacle, before the representation with all its glaringly illuminated and well-hidden aspects and effects, there is a multiplicity in whose folds music plays. Before the first beat, there was already a cigarette with the cleaning crew after the soundcheck, a smile exchanged while waiting for the entrance, an exuberance in anticipation, a desire from all directions and in all directions, a murmur when something moves on stage, a wave of a hand from back there, together lurking for the return of the desiring machine. And all this waiting and awaiting, lurking and harking, being eager and braced is itself already part of music, a cog in a social machine, this bulging nothing-ness, multiplicity. And before that, the rehearsal, the sociality of the rehearsal room, another such social machine, actually completely independent of whether there might be a show at some point, and to that extent a performance in itself. An endurance performance, without needing much endurance: time-forgetting times, day and night, sprawling into sessions, undisciplined offshoots of a semi-disciplined practice, and with changing personnel – one person leaves, three others come from other rehearsal rooms, and the change between instruments joins the change between playing and listening, in the best case all at the same time, and already it's over again with the sharp division between active and passive, solo and accompaniment, making music and letting music be made.

So music always plays before the rehearsal begins, before the show begins, before the music begins to play. Even if their voices remain minor, half-loud in undertones, this music plays in many layers, drawing fine lines, down to the smallest details, into the farthest folds of multiplicity. Its sociality is multilayered and resists appropriation and unification. Its anthem is counter-song, backtalk, echoing dissonance, hypophony, and it draws a line of turbidity and disturbance, creates whirl, trouble, turbulence. Instead of the symphony, a hypophonic disorder, instead of the hymn conducted by someone to someone, an antiphonal-orgic orchestra without direction; and no one really knows who belongs to it and who doesn't, where the stage is and where the audience, and when the music will have begun to play.

6

Of Joints, Disjointures, and Subjunctures

No doubt, the world is out of joint, even today, still or anew again and again. While ubiquitous normalization drives the longing for normality, the normal can be produced less and less. Increasingly violent border regimes, new and not so new forms of slavery and radical exploitation, multiple crises, wars and civil wars, fascism, social isolation, enormous expansion of anxiety and depression. In this way the world is out of joint.

But today, at the same time, there is the problem that everything joins too well. No longer simply enjoined in a vertical, authoritarian injunction, as docile character and subservient subject, but also joining in the techno-regimes and self-government of machinic capitalism. Everything goes smoothly, at least in transhumanist fantasy. Endlessly and subjectlessly, joining assemblages fit into the wandering joints. In smooth modulations and gapless alignments, routines run like clockwork, disposability endures. Access becomes totalized, and more and more detailed. And even if the joints wander, different things adapt to each other, in modulations without gaps. No longer joining into one big picture, but rather adapting to the respective situation; no longer only vertically joined, but joined from all sides. Compatible and spectrally distributed, the joints and self-joinings of compliant conduct undulate.

Life in the joints is a well-behaved, a convenient, a bland life – if it weren't for these peaks of agitation, if it weren't for the fear of being thrown out of joint. But even affects like rage, indignation and stubbornness join to this joining, following their logic of modulating the deviant. And so the joints close; as filter bubbles they become airtight self-amplifiers, their contents variations of the same old thing, conformations to themselves. Thus they tend to become sealed-off feedback loops and dump joints, dull joints, rage joints, self-reinforcing rubber cells and resonance spaces between lethargy and indignation.

These joinings occur beyond the separation of virtual and real spaces: it would be a gross underestimation to understand hate as a "real" and individual affect, as the authentic affect of an individual who merely uses social networks as platforms for spreading this affect. On the leash of corporate social media, modes of conduct emerge with affects far beyond individual and instrumental use, with contagions, baiting masses, and swarms of hate. At the same time, the fascistoid affections and effects of unification in dense gatherings, from the backroom as a historical echo chamber to populist rallies and fascist rackets, are by no means a thing of the past. It is precisely the interaction of different social spaces that develops such explosiveness, even on contested streets and in the remnants of public space.

How can other affects take space, beyond aggression and hate speech, shaming and cyberbullying, stalking and harassment? What does it mean today to be *enragé*es, indigné*es, indignad*s*? How can the joints of rage be countered by a vulnerable-caring wildness, a queer-feminist multiplicity of care? How do affection and affectability enter the usages of resistance and insurrection?

First and foremost immanently, in the same joints of machinic capitalism, precisely because in production and reproduction we ourselves are parts of the flow and the breakdown of the machines. Right here, in rampant flows and cruel stagnations, in joints and disjoinings, something is also stirring that cannot be joined in this way. After the Middle High German word *unvuoge* we can call it *Unfuge*, disjointure: that which cannot be made disposable in its entirety, not in such a way; that which is before violence and at the same time is pursued by this violence. Disjointure is not only grammatically but also often empirically feminine, before patriarchal violence and its threat, but definitely deviant, transverse to normalization, never quite alone, many and manifold, closer to asignificance and affection than to aggression against something or someone in particular. The usages of disjointure are indecent behavior, soft-infamous unrest, dangerous-insubordinate counter-conduct, ungovernability, refusal of government and self-government.

Disjointure is not an individual figure of disobedience, a character to be educated, but an always asymmetrical-unbalanced relation and dividual destitution. It is a funked-out spark that leaps beyond human conditions, a revolt of things, a revolt with the things, with the living beings, with the machines. Not joining in the joints of rage, but disjoining them like its self, the disjointure is unruly in its relation to the environment, and its ungovernable sociality shapes the subjuncture. When disjoining the self, the disjointure lets itself fall into multiplicity, into the subjuncture, which it co-constitutes in the disjoining of the self.

The subjuncture does not join the joints. The subjuncture does not join the disjointures. When the disjointures are joined, the subjuncture collapses. When the joints do not join, when they become disjointures, the subjuncture surrounds and traverses them at the same time. It turns, inverts, reverses the joints. It transforms the joints. Constituted in the self-disjoining of the disjointures, the subjuncture mutates with them and with the joints.

The subjuncture is not merely around; it is below, and it is across, a capacity for transmutation. It does not enclose, like walls enclose a castle or troops laying siege enclose the same castle. It does not envelop, is not a chamber, immurement, isolation. It is a fraying territory of care in which creatures of all kinds, animals, spirits, bodies, machines, things, do not exist by blood and soil and being born, or by property and law and individuality, but subsist through their subsistence.

The subjuncture subjoins by traversing. It underlies by being immanent. It corresponds to an *oikos* that goes beyond classical notions of ecology. Subjoining ecology is far from being a single-issue playground of soft-green actors. The climate catastrophe shows us to what degree today environmental issues are transversal. In this sense, ecology means a perspective that focuses on complex compositions of surrounds: surrounds that are not understood as something external, something that envelops and encloses the world, but rather as transversally traversing the world.

As far as multiplicity is concerned, a subjoining form of ecology is not limited to lamentations about species extinction or a simple praise of biodiversity. If such praise is limited to identifying and counting species, it remains as similarly reductive as the social ideal of diversity premised on the inclusion and representation of "minorities." Multiplicity in the subjuncture is not so much biodiversity in the sense of a countable accumulation of species. It is not content to count and tick off individual species, but cares for the dividual relations between them, their surrounds. Multiplicity in the subjuncture is the flows, the streams, the middles, the uncountable bio-multiplicity of life.

Against this background, ecological activism must not only think ecology transversally; the struggles in the subjuncture must be conceived in the same transversal way. Even in the face of huge urgencies, the multiple crises can only be tackled if they are thought and discussed in all their complexity, and without giving way to drastic and reductive political marketing. When the extinction of humanity is predicted and a generation calls itself the last, the argument seems large and universal, its tone eschatological. But there is a multiple reductionism behind it: in a sense, a new principal contradiction is introduced here, which is no longer the contradiction of labor and capital, as in the nineteenth century, but the contradiction of climate revolution and nation-states. Here, not only is the transversality of struggles reduced to one main contradiction, without taking into account the many axes of oppression and the asymmetries involved, but also the problem and its solution are projected onto nation-states. These may be important actors in the struggle against the multiple crises, but a fixation on states will not help us to bring them closer to a solution. Far beyond the limits of any nation-state, in machinic capitalism there is no way of reordering things in a form which does not consider its machinic flows and transversal dimensions and geopolitical gradations. Finally, the salvation of the species and of "human civilization" is also strangely abstract and focused on the future, in a paradoxical overlap also with longtermist ideology, which promises to save humanity with the help of technology by relocating it to Mars, and more generally to outer space, not bothering about people in the here and now, their forms of subsistence and their subsistential territories.

Against all this, one can only recall again and again the marvelous complexity and multiplicity inherent in less simplistic ways of struggling, including ecological struggles, struggles that are transversal, condividual, and unruly. Beyond individuality and in the mode of condivision, indignation and rage leave the rage joints, with all their malice, hatred, and shaming. When the joints get out of joint, condivision releases the disjointures, and the caring subjuncture becomes their social terrain. Down here everything is disposable, down here nothing joins.

7

Of Subsistence and the Subsisting

Where something comes into being and stands and subsists, something else must come into being and stand and subsist at its side, in it and around it. In scholastic philosophy, subsistence is that by which something is. Everything that subsists has its own subsistence, which is in it and underlies it. Where something subsists, its subsistence is at its side. Subsistence is neither individual nor universal existence nor substance; it does not unify or generalize subsisting things but affirms and preserves them specifically in their multiplicity.

Affirming this multiplicity of the subsisting does not mean uncritically accepting whatever happens in it; it means transforming the deaf eavesdropping attack from above and outside into a differentiating listening with others. In the subjuncture the things do not make themselves audible to us, but mutual listening makes the subjuncture. Those who populate it listen together, listen to each other, listen around, listen and lurk, in all the ambivalence between neighborly control and subsistential care, sometimes both at the same time. Preserving the multiplicity of the subsisting does not mean keeping it the same for ever and ever, conserving it or embalming it; it means caring for the subjuncture, insisting on its multiplicity of care, making its manifold care relations persistent and becoming persistent with them. Preservation means staying, staying with multiplicity: coal staying in the ground, occupations resisting eviction, social machines staying in the turbid.

Subsistence causes the concretion of the subsisting; it underlies the subsisting, according to the meaning of the Latin *sub-sistere*, yet not like a general ground but as the specific subsistence of a co-emergent subsisting. Thus, in the turn to immanence of scholastic philosophy, the subsisting does not arise by multiplication from a one; it has its being not from an outside, from a substance, but from the subsistence that is in it, that pervades and immanently surrounds it. Conversely, a subsistence is not in several, but only in one subsisting. A single subsistence "makes" only a single subsisting. Neither ground nor origin, subsistence as surround and subjuncture is in and under and around the subsisting.

Building on classical feminist research on the economy of subsistence, and opening it into the queer, subsistence becomes an antidote to substantialist-essentialist positions that elevate the soil, imagining *terra* as inherited, whether as property, patriarchal lineage, or supratemporal belonging. Territory and territoriality come into play here not as a figure of blood and soil, but as a ritornello-like movement, as rhythmic repetition and return, milieu and material earth constituting the subsistential territory – a territory in which things, machines, spirits, living beings live side by side, with each other and apart, in subsistential division and disposability.

The economy of subsistence is not a necessity-driven economy of self-sufficiency, of staying for oneself, of self-preservation, coming from scarcity and determined by necessity. It does not reproduce the idea of pre-modern patriarchal forms of subsistence economy outside of the cities. It implies a queer-feminist form of care economy, present in all kinds of ephemera, in the least capitalized and colonized rural areas, but also in the middle of the eye of urban densification, in the holes of metropolitan agglomerations, starting from the subsistence of wild care in the block, in the neighborhood, in the barrio.

Beneath the smooth, smart, attractive surfaces there is something that does not fit, that is not so attractive, not so smart and not so smooth. The subsistential territory is not the territory of the existence of individuals; it is the subjuncture in which subsisting is divided dividually. It has no definite extension, it is territory at all scales, from the repurposing of the artifacts of street furniture to the spontaneous meeting at the corner and its rhythmic repetition, to the assemblage of social places in the neighborhood, grocery store, inn, supermarket, playground, park, and bookstore. The subsistential territory is the field of immanence, never a closed and enclosed territory, and never finished, its lines always drawing it further and shifting its borders. It is down here, outside, in the middle of things, amid animals, plants, and architectures in their re- and deterritorializations and struggles for territory.

The economy of subsistence breaks through the logic of possessive individualism. The asymmetrical multiplicity of care relations in the production of subjoining sociality does not start from individuals and does not have an individualizing effect. In contrast to its reductive translation as self-sufficiency and self-preservation, it does not revolve around a self. It is not clientelistic or top-down organized, not totalizing or communitarian, but condividual. With this concept of subsistence, care shifts from the caring, feminized subject and its identification of individual interest and need, to dividual desire. Subsistence here means being traversed by the dividual lines that move through things, bodies, ghosts, through space and time. In this way, it also loses the anthropocentric connotation that resonates in one-sided terms such as concern and empathy, and focuses instead on dividual desire and the machinic flows between and through things.

The search for the place of the sub- in subsistence leads in all possible directions; down there perhaps, but not into the depth, not to the bottom, not into the abyss. And certainly there is no subsoil below the bottom, only a two-dimensional expansion of the plane of immanence, drawing the dividual lines that make and make up and change the territory. The sub- in subsistence is that which is emerging and imposing itself both down here and all around. Down here is where we dig up the grounds, dig on both sides of the surface. Down, yes, but also suspending the relation of up and down. From the subsistential-subsisting point of view there is no above, and even the image of the two sides of a surface is too simple, missing the many folds of the below.

8

Of Caring Company, Propertyless Occupation, and Poor Possession

When it comes to finding ways out of the seemingly all-encompassing economy of machinic capitalism, least helpful are grandiloquent speeches, simple solutions, and grand plans. Not only because the macro-alternatives of modernity have historically, without exception and to this day, deformed into authoritarian forms of government and state, but also because the nets are becoming ever more tightly meshed, the joints ever more narrowly joined, and the capitalist appropriations, cooptations, and valorizations ever faster and without gaps.

Against this background, it is obvious that economic, social, and political experiments need not be tested according to the dichotomous logic of micro and macro scalings. The dividual search movement does not so much address the question of possible scale as pursue procedures bent on the radical transformation of usages, expanding the immanence field along with its lines, allowing them to be carried along in its middle, whirling, blocking, and flowing towards the condividual revolution.

Care is a prudent merchant. Instead of ruthlessly exploiting and ceaselessly appropriating things, people, and selves, caring prudence prefers use in the sense of usufruct, keeping caring company with things. It is a matter of undirected circumspection in the subjuncture, while at the same time paying specific attention to specific things, machines, and living beings; a matter of continuous negotiation of possession and occupation, a disjoining and rejoining of property as dividual division. Things, bodies, spirits, and machines do not have to be valorized, appropriated, or forced to comply. Without disregarding the violence of class relations, dividual division disjoins property, seeking to erase the markings left by its owners. It does not erase them completely, but renders them diffuse, dark, turbid enough to occupy the territory differently, to be possessed by it and by its ghosts, not to count it in occupying it, but to make it a subsistential territory for a time.

For a queer-feminist economy of subsistence, the transformation of passive-aggressive, comfortable-compliant, or simply exploitative usages into caring-dividual usages is central: things can be used with care, without taking them away from others. This is a use that does not fall back on the legal title of property; a use which, despite the ordering of things through property, focuses rather on the not-so-ordered, caring use of things, working with the things, in co-formity.

Caring usage is a mode of use that does not abuse or consume. Less in the sense of leaving a portion for others, finely measured and counted, made disposable for successive use, one by one, divided also according to the subject and object of use. Rather in the double sense of enjoying: enjoyment as usufruct, the caring use of things, machines, surrounds, avoiding or disjoining property; but also a versatile enjoyment as the dividual production of desire. Caring usage is more than just usance, more than tentative habit, and more than one kind of usage among many. It is a conduct and mode of existence, insofar as care becomes dividual desire and permeates everyday life.

Against the background of a caring and co-forming approach to things, occupation does not mean appropriation. Perhaps everything is already appropriated, but occupation plays with other tunings than that of appropriation. Nowhere is a no man's land if we listen to what is already there. To occupy means to listen, to hear the subjuncture and, in hearing it, to transform it, retune it. Maintaining occupation requires *détournement*, a re-functioning of what is already there, be it a park bench or a wasteland, a club or a folk festival, a street sign or a house wall, a desolate telephone booth or an empty sky-scraper.

And even in possession there is still something of a defection from possession, of making the multiplicity of the appropriated audible again, of making it sound, of reusing possession with others, using it differently, in caring company and poor possession. This requires a different form of disposability than the kind which is central to machinic capitalism: not the dispos-ability of algorithmic search movements, mass data mining, and colonizing accumulation, but rather a practice of making disposable, of placing at disposal, of disjoining possession.

The deviant economy of caring company, occupation, and poor possession does not promise an ideal world, a classless society, or a zone cleansed of asymmetries. Without sublating them, it can name violence and denounce domination, it can shift the asymmetries. At the same time, it can also care for and expand its wild mix, its blend of undisposability, indignation, and disobedience, and of other forms of disposability, the councils in subjuncture: neighborhood associations, cine-clubs, anti-eviction platforms, reading groups, anti-racist alliances, feminist strike committees, orgic cooperatives. All too often, overwhelmed and abandoned by co-formity, we are doomed to failure in face of the tension between occupation and possession, and yet we do not cease to draw the lines, to surround the property, to brace the subsistential territory anew every day, disjoining possession and self-appropriation in the rhythm of caring company, so that even the last possession recalls the multiplicity from which it comes.

9

Of Technecologies and Transverses

Ecology cannot be limited to a return to nature, to degrowth, to the renunciation of consumption and the stopping of the machines; it must bring forth completely new usages in the middle of what is there, be it ruins or newly blooming meadows or landscapes situated between virtual and real. There are reasons for alarmism as there are for reformism, but there are many more reasons for condividual revolution.

Precisely because the machinic aspects of our lives, in all their class and geopolitical gradations, have such a significant effect on ways of life and social assemblages, ecology, too, must be read machinically, beyond any dichotomy of technology and nature. This is what the term technecology stands for. It does not simply imply technology as an instrument of ecological transformation, or the salvation of ecologies as a magical effect of techno-fixes; nor does it imply a subsequent fusion of technology and ecology; rather, it emphasizes the all-round joining of the ecological and the machinic.

This joining is condensed in the everyday technologies of ecological activism. For example in the now routine livestreaming of actions, often documenting the brutal police repression, but more importantly documenting the activists' own actions and their resistant character: from the occupations of mines and forests and various practices of blockade, to the use of walkie-talkies, video cameras, and drones to monitor illegal mining activities in rainforests and indigenous territories. As a habitual element of ecological struggles, this use of low-tech means and everyday technologies continues to point beyond the normalized dichotomy of nature and technology.

In this turn away from the anti-technological, ecological activism can also overcome its localist limitations. For all the sensible critiques of cruises, round-the-world ‘ trips, weekend flights, and other consumerist forms of traveling, demands for extreme restrictions on travel and freedom of movement often seem socially and politically counterproductive. They can be countered by blended practices that – whether they involve high or low tech – cross the old divide between local and global anew. Transversal machines of farnearness emerge precisely in the most diverse combinations of network-based communication and assemblies in real space.

If we want to combat the interlocking forms of techno-authoritarianism and machinic subservience, new usages and ecologies are needed that cannot be separated from technological developments. Antidotes to the new forms of techno-government will not be found in anti-technological retreat and absolute machinic withdrawal, nor in attempts at bureaucratic containment, but only in the invention of machinic usages that consider the surround and sociality, modes of conduct and technologies, in connection with one another. Against the socio-narcissism of corporate social media, these machinic-ecological usages will multiply technecologies, bracing and joining technical and social machines.

If technecological usages flee machinic subservience in all spheres of life, they nevertheless persist in the middle of the machines, with the machines, in co-formity with machines. This middle of the machines does not imply any transhuman fantasy of the human body fused with technology, nor the fiction of sentient and intelligent androids; rather, it envisions a human-machinic soft-ware that promotes technopolitics not as a territory of hate and malice, not as a masculinist geek sport, but as a wild softness in equally softly subjoining machines. This is the basis of new forms of ecology: a softness that also concerns the thing-world, the things of the sur-round, in the broadest sense.

Technecological usages imply new joinings, permeable subjunctures, porous, fraying social ecologies and techno-milieus. Insofar as they are and remain porous, they can avoid becom-ing self-amplifiers, self-sustaining eco-bubbles, techno-chambers. Sometimes it may be tactically appropriate to construct temporary techno-autonomous zones that constitute themselves as local platforms. But translocality and machinic-ecological connectivity – the capacity to append and connect – remain central.

The technecological questioning of property relations calls for a renewed "expropriation of the expropriators," for the re-expropriation or counter-expropriation of those who have appropriated and continue to appropriate the transversal intellect across the world wide web and corporate social media. All "intellectual property" calls for its liberation. It also calls for a liquidation of the monopolies over the platforms themselves and the codes they apply. But even more important than the expropriation of the expropriators and the liberation of the codes is the invention of new machines and data economies capable of confronting the appropriation processes of recent decades, subjoining them in apposition in order to undermine them and render them worthless. If they succeed in this, one of their most important characteristics will be their implementation with thorns, barbs, and sharp edges, ensuring that they cannot be so easily expropriated as so much has been before, so that their appropriation becomes impossible or at least entails proper damage.

The exploitative form of corporate social media has become more and more evident in recent years. Since their software is proprietary and their code is kept secret, they cannot be changed by users. Monopolistic tendencies and clear dominances in their application sectors determine the spheres of influence of the individual players. They operate in total isolation, offering no opportunities for exchange with other networks. Their barely concealed economic function lies in the colonization of data spaces and the extraction of data and protocols, without regard for the work of the many involved in data production. Their content-related and ethical positions show corporate social media – despite or because of their appeals to openness, which essentially amount to machinic appropriation processes – to be politically problematic in a narrower sense as well.

Alternative projects cannot be limited to preventive appropriation controls, but must develop new forms of caring use, propertyless occupation, and poor possession. In the technecological realm, one such new form emerged a few years ago as the fediverse – an assemblage of independent and decentralized social networks, microblogging sites and publishing platforms, the best-known of which is Mastodon. The so-called fediverse "instances," often of very different size, are set up on their own servers and are independent of each other, but they can also interact and link up with other instances at any time. This form of federation and interoperability in the fediverse, along with its consistent use of free software and involvement of users in self-organization, is a huge step forward compared to corporate social media with their massive restrictions and commercial interests.

An important issue arising out of the still relatively short history of net culture is the need to consider, alongside forms of coupling and bracing, forms of decoupling, blocking, and defederation. In the fediverse, this can apply to individual users who defy the respective codes of conduct, but more generally it concerns two forms of situated decoupling in response to large-scale attacks: on the one hand, resisting all forms of fascist, sexist, racist or far-right groups with identitarian ideologies opposed to the principle of the federation itself; on the other hand, resisting corporate social media in their bid to swallow up by cooptation or takeover everything that cannot be displaced by competition. Such processes of decoupling and rupturing have also often been associated with understanding how deeply net-cultural discourses in particular were, and in some cases still are, informed by the liberal ideologemes of free speech, openness, and universality.

In contrast, the fediverse thinking is shaped by radical inclusion and opt-in rather than opt-out solutions, by situated opening and closing protocols, and by the interoperability of platforms. Its starting point is the instance model: the instance as one manifestation of many coexisting instances can be conceived and maneuvered in different ways. Instances can have very tightly formulated or very elaborate protocols and codes of conduct, they can be strongly or weakly moderated, and the degree of user involvement in the management of a platform can vary greatly.

This variability and multiplicity is also a prerequisite for the possible further development of the fediverse beyond federation. In classical conceptions, federation refers to the structure of a political body; in relation to the fediverse, it entails the union of different decentralized units, be they networks, platforms, or their instances. From a technecological point of view, however, the same structure could be understood differently: no longer as a linking of points in a network or as primary instances connecting on a secondary stage, no longer as a fediverse only, but as a transverse.

In this perspective, the translocal traffic of transversal machines emerges not from the tracing of connecting lines between pre-existent points, but simultaneously with the concrete, local, situated machines. There is no secondary connection, no network or actor–network relationship, but rather farnearness, the parallel emergence of technopolitical subsistence and subsisting machines. Instances are then not antecedent parts, as points in a network, but manifold situated territories. For these instances of reterritorialization the transverse is not a superior instance, but a transversal machine, situated between the instances and traversing them, dividually distributed and ever further dividing.

Technecological transverses and their alternative infrastructures are ultimately also involved in facilitating condividual compositions. The transverse is not a metaverse enclosing its immersive world in the corporate social medium. Nor is it an omniverse whose cosmos is limited to the parallel world of artificial intelligence, without people and matter. However, transforming the manic flows of desire in the anti-social networks of machinic capitalism requires more than simply changing its infrastructure. It requires joining the infrastructural conditions of the fedi-verse with dividual usages, with social machines and dividual-machinic ways of life. It requires a disruption of the manic flows, and with it the invention of a co-formity that turns on desiring machines: machinic and yet not manic.

Of Softness, Unmunt, and Minor Masculinity

In the queer mysticism of the European High Middle Ages, softness and sweetness were terms that concerned, on the one hand, relationships between women, but also, and above all, the relationship of female mystics to masculinely coded deities; as, for example, in the soft opening of a farnear divinity, or in the fact that the relationship between the divine friend and the femininely connoted soul is without domination. Sweetness, tenderness, and softness here refer less to the character traits of a subject than to ways of relating, to affections rather than affects.

This understanding of softness in relationship was not a romantic glorification, but a response precisely to the radical subjugation of women, for whom forms of direct resistance were almost completely unavailable. *Douceur* and *suavitas*, sweetness and softness, are here markers of unruliness, of a form of disobedience based precisely on this material given. In taking up and affirming what was there anyway – softness as vulnerability – unruly women practiced a kind of inverse obedience in relationship with the divine without ecclesiastical mediation, as a usage of disobedience that arose in self-disjoining.

Though queer *avant la lettre*, what was missing in these narratives of softness and sweetness – and what is becoming more and more urgent today in the face of exacerbations of male violence, machismo and feminicide, rigid heteronormativity and gender binarity, and new masculinisms in authoritarianism and war – are other conceptions of masculinity. Of a masculinity that refuses domination, that does not want to practice it, that is not fit to be head of the household, not fit for the master's, the guardian's, *Munt* power over all other persons living therein, as old Germanic law would have it. A masculinity that remains *Un-Munt*, immature and unwilling to become mature. This masculinity in the form of unmunt never claims the normality of coming of age. It is

neither willing to exercise nor capable of domination, appropriation, and possession. It remains
minor, underage, a minor masculinity, a masculinity in minor life.

You can never become man. And where there
is no path towards becoming, it becomes a question of unlearning masculinity as an identity. A
ruse here, a circumlocution there. The delicate
task of a minor masculinity is to remain mut-
able, adapting to different surrounds, mutating
with them, in a polytropic, zealous mutation up
to assimilation, until any goal of approximation
seems to have been lost. When the multiplicity
of objects grows into immensity, the subjects
of similarity become blurred, and the surround
is too confused for one becoming same with it.
Minor masculinity is undirected assimilation,
always too bad, never quite successful, all-around
failing-failed assimilation, approximation, too
minor to end in the same.

In all its twists and turns, minor masculinity
nevertheless seeks its ways, from case to case, without any general solution, without legal certainty.
Its machinations are groundless and all-round;
its betrayal is a flight from authenticity, from
sedentarism and the filiation of father and son. It

requires a defection from binarity and a fidelity to all things; a radical affirmation in becoming similar to the things of the subjuncture, a refusal of objectification, a co-formity with things. In the middle of things, minor masculinity is at the same time disloyalty towards its "own" gender and loyalty towards all possible sides.

The unmunt of minor masculinity exists before the guardian and lets him be. It flees his protection, which is domination, appropriation, and permanent cooptation. Unprotected, without paternal protection, it is vulnerable, fragile, but never quite alone. It remains unfit for all ownership, content with use, occupation, and indwelling, not even owning itself, possessed by the many, by the inauthentic spirits, by the vocal kin in unmunt. It refuses to become a sovereign subject that detaches itself from the guardian's *Munt,* from maintaining its own *Munt* power, a power in turn based on the devaluation and exclusion of everything that is minor, not white, not human, not male. It persists in immaturity, in its unwillingness to arrive at the standard measure, to become a man of age, a real man, a big man.

At the same time as affirming and insisting on the capacity of softness, however, unmunt transforms the patriarchal role of protection-giving, governing, and controlling into something else. Unmunt becomes uncompliant usage, non-normalizable, not disposable to the joint and right of the master and guardian, and not even to mature self-government. It develops caring usages beyond anthropocentric perspectives, in soft, sweet, affective relations with all kinds of critters, with plants and animals, with technical apparatuses and thing-worlds. All this makes up the human-machinic soft-ware, its softly subjoining masculinity caring immaturely for dividual desire and mutual machines of affection.

II

Of Becoming Nothing

And when they object: "But in view of the multiple crises of this world, in view of the violence, in view of the suffering, where is the negation in this making of multiplicity, the negativity, where is the critique in all this?," then don't say no, not the negative again as power of sublation, not critique again as all too German, and be it anti-German laziness of thought. Rather say yes, negation, critique, capacity of the negative, all this and much more is included in the differentiation and complication of multiplicity in becoming nothing.

And instead of thesis and antithesis a little apposition; instead of sublation a sea of love; instead of binarisms an unidentifiable noise; until critique is infinite differentiation and negation is becoming nothing. Thinking to stare into nothingness, a gaze turns to seeing: not simply seeing nothing or even nothingness, but seeing turbidity, which sometimes becomes brighter, and even then ever not quite. Nothingness is the turbid, the confused, and the scattered. What can be seen is infinitely many, multitudes, multiplicity.

If in machinic capitalism we are obsessed with possessive individualism and self-government, at the same time marked by a violent deindividuation, if where there is social intercourse we see only competition, if where socio-psychic problems spread we only sense a necessary self-optimization, then we have to defect from the regime of joining. More than the Franciscan idea of giving away all one's property, insofar as one has any, this defection entails a dividual desertion from one's own, from one's self, a self-disjoining.

It is precisely in the joinings of machinic capitalism that we comply in self-government, becoming subservient by governing ourselves. Self-joining is production of the self, and self-government the perpetual repetition of this joining, as a fabrication and optimization of the self set in an infinite series. Here it is no longer enough to turn against the state or the government or the capitalist actors who exploit us. Without becoming self-destructive, we must also turn against an enjoined and subservient self – disempowering self-empowerment, rejecting self-management, leaving self-determination indeterminate wherever it involves machinic techniques of the self. The first requirement in resisting appropriation is to lose oneself, to let the self go, to lose one's composure, to be beside oneself, to defect from ownership of oneself – turning away from the self as something to be possessed and constantly improved, to become unpossessed, unmeasurable, unsettlable, and at the same time possessed by a multiplicity of spirits and things.

Self-disjoining is not nihilism, nor absolute deterritorialization, nor extinction or self-dissolution, nor absorption in God; it is, on the contrary, a weapon against self-government, a revolt of the joined, disjoining the extremely jointed and enjoined machinic-capitalist conditions. Resisting a subservient life on the leash, disjoining the self means breaking this sticky bond of joints. When the constant production and improvement of the self in machinic flows leads to an ever more expansive subservience and disposability, the mystical practice of *excessus mentis* as an excess leading out of the self becomes a machinic-materialist practice of defecting from the joining, of undoing the specific form of disposability in machinic capitalism. This self-disjoining is a co-emergent condition of transmutation in becoming similar and co-formed, finally also a condition of virtual assembly.

Self-disjoining is emptying, becoming nothing, but there is no emptiness in nothing, no empty nothing, only a divided bounty, multitude, multiplicity of nothing. Becoming nothing is becoming, which is at the same time letting go, letting go of the self, but also being attracted by farnearness, attracted to gathering and bracing, to other ways of joining. And again the middle voice comes into play: becoming nothing is active and passive at the same time, a mystical letting go, letting oneself be subjoined in disjoining, falling into the middle, into multiplicity.

Mystically understood, nothingness is a sea of love, the sea into which all rivers, all waters, all souls feed, but not as a great and final sublation and dissolution into an ever-the-same mass. The rivers, the waters, the souls lose their names, their selves, their individual peculiarities, and yet they remain specific parts of the multiplicity. Drops, waves, currents, fed by boundless inflows, roam through this sea of multiplicity, drifting and falling, sinking and flowing, mutating into abundance, overflow, excess. It is probably more helpful to imagine this sea not as one single huge varnish over the ever-same immanence, but rather at all scales, as larger and smaller seas, lakes, ponds, puddles, as many middles and milieus.

Becoming nothing is not negation or nihilism, but the affirmation of a life that lets itself fall into multiplicity, into the mutual transformation of the disjoined self and nothing: this mystical-materialistic transmutation of the subjunctures, never arriving at nothing, but remaining a continuous and multifaceted becoming in multiplicity.

12

Of Transversal Intellect

The bourgeois public sphere, like the concept of the public sphere in general, is not the contrary of the corporate social media bubble, since it has itself always been bubble-like. Colonial, Eurocentric, positing itself as universal, this public sphere encompassed the educated bourgeois milieu, which defined itself through exclusions in all directions, culminating in the intellectual who, in his liberality, read both *Le Monde* and *Libération*, *taz* and *Frankfurter Allgemeine*, *The Times* and *The Guardian* every day. During its decline in the 1980s and 1990s, the bourgeois public sphere produced extreme distortions of its intellectual figures. These media intellectuals – servile remnants of the idea of the public intellectual and direct precursors of today's bubble intellectuals – were pure functionaries of the bourgeois media, neatly conforming to its frame as soon as they were asked onto any public stage.

Since the mid-1980s, post-operaist philosophy has proposed an interpretation of structural transformation in which the public sphere moves from the political into the realms of production, thus "depoliticizing" itself in a specific sense. It is capitalist production that now takes on the structure of the public sphere, increasingly assuming the modulation of social cooperation and of an intellect that has become subservient. Cooperation, coordination, and communication become central moments of production, and thus of capitalist valorization. While the direct negotiation of common affairs tends to take place only in the realm of labor and the real and virtual spaces it determines, the dimension of the public sphere as a site of bourgeois political action tends to disappear.

The "Western" institutions of culture and education, so central to the construction of the public sphere, are being completely transformed in machinic capitalism. More and more, thinking and publishing are pressed into the logic of individuality and property, protected as intellectual property and copyrighted, no matter what individual authors might have to say about it. And this legal logic is still at work in the liberal form of the creative commons. The dividual machinations of thought that transcend and subvert the individual mind have been striated, stratified, and institutionalized for many centuries. Since its foundation, the institution of the university has mainly served to secure and expand domination. After a relatively short phase in the years after 1968, which saw pedagogical and organizational experiments in self-administration and the radical reform of universities, this fundamental orientation of the university as servant of domination is back in all its fullness. What is new are the extreme transformations of educational institutions in their joinings according to the rules of machinic capitalism, with the economic valorizability and disposability of knowledge now supreme principles. The stratified academic institution has gridded itself inwardly and closed itself off outwardly, surrendering thought to the laws of a thoroughly valorized system of knowledge production: screening and measuring at all levels; constant increases in tuition fees, with class-specific exclusions and student indebtedness as direct consequences; fragmentation of study time as a result of modularization; extreme hierarchization of research and teaching; peer review as a process of inclusion and exclusion; growing intrusion of corporations and foundations into educational institutions; and the simultaneous expansion of university business into real estate markets, infrastructure policy, and global franchising. The university, then, is obviously not an overly welcoming place, and yet, or precisely because of this, it is worth pursuing the double desertion that has arguably accompanied it since its origins: the desertion within the institution, with the development of minor monsters that appropriate its interstices, transversal to the institutional structures and antagonisms; but the desertion also in the founding of self-organized formations of knowledge production.

These forms of desertion also occurred in the 1990s and 2000s, contemporaneously with the dissolution of the bourgeois public sphere and its institutions. In different parts of Europe and the Americas, lively discursive connections between political theory and activism emerged, especially in the cultural field. This critical and radical polyphony generated productive discursive shifts, with new conceptualizations and undisciplined experiments in the forms of knowledge production. As bracings of social movements and knowledge production, they moved not only in the midst of a boom in conferences, publications, and exhibitions in the fields of art and cultural studies, but also in the midst of the struggles that shaped the public spaces and discourses of the time – the alter-globalization movement, no-border networks, pink and silver blocs, mayday movements, among many others.

From Reclaim the Streets in the 1990s, to the *piqueteros* and *escraches* in Argentina, to the plaza occupations of the 2010s, the public sphere seemed to be returning from capitalist production to its mythical arena, the center of the city. This time, however, as a very material practice, and in all its class multiplicity; beyond any invocation of the bourgeois public sphere, these movements insisted that the smooth spaces of urban centers as touristic and privatized spheres had lost even the last semblance of being public space.

The figure of the "bourgeois intellectual" also seemed to be off the table for a while. In the spring of 2011, collective intelligences and public intellects emerged in Tunisia, Egypt, and Spain, and even when prominent intellectuals appeared at Occupy Wall Street in New York's Zuccotti Park, their invasive individuality was thwarted by the manifold instrument of the human microphone: in the absence of technical amplification, their speeches were amplified phrase by phrase through choral repetition for the whole assembly and to all corners of the park. Here, micro-amplification and the multiplication of voices, even when speaking the same thing, functioned as a practice of radical polyphony: one voice supported the speaker with affirming hand signs; the next, repeating the speaker's last sentence, declared dissent with other hand signs, while a third turned away from the speaker, to better ensure the "neutral" amplifier function for the bystanders. Making multiplicity meant unfolding multiplicity, transversalizing the intellect *in actu*, letting it become dividual.

It is as an effect of the intensification of machinic-capitalist conditions, ecological crisis, pandemic and war, that these political movements have also decayed in recent years, or else let themselves fall into other forms that are not yet precisely discernible today. This has occurred not solely as a consequence of repression by reactionary media and authoritarian state apparatuses; often the movements simply imploded, lacking connection to social machines, thereby increasing the cannibalization and dichotomization of multiplicity.

While it looked for a while as if the ever new New Philosophers, public intellectuals, and media intellectuals were losing relevance – partly thanks to their own idiosyncrasies, but also due to the rise of radical critical movements like Kanak Attack, the international women's universities, Edu-factory, Onda Anomala, Uni brennt, and many more – it now seems as if the figure of the idiosyncratic intellectual is simply returning in a different form, in different places. The discursive reach that used to be achieved by newspapers, radio, and television is now being established through corporate social media platforms and messenger channels. As a result, along with the influencer model, an intellectual figure has been pushing its way into media discourse for some time, becoming known in German-speaking countries by the name "Querdenker." As querulous "contrarian thinkers" and propagandists of extreme identitarian ideologies, they often practice discursive violence *ad personam* against minority groups. Climate change deniers, Covid deniers, and paranoid conspiracy theorists may perform their own minority, but in truth they attack minorities in asymmetrical constellations. Renitence and resilience are close to each other here: Seeing themselves as nonconformist, they serve their scenes compliantly. With chatbot swarms, they conform in the joints of rage, producing whatever promises them attention, impact, and appeal. Far more than just narcissism and chaotic incoherence, this form of communication combines reactionary enunciations with algorithmic searches for majorities.

Against the transformations of machinic capitalism and its contribution to the expansion of such extreme right-wing positions and ideologies, a different kind of thought is needed, one radically non-individual and with a different focus on knowledge production to that of the traditional university or classical forms of intellectuality. Intellect here is always more than a faculty individually possessed that enters into discussion with other individual intellects in a rationally deliberative or polemical manner. It is a collective intelligence or general intellect, long before any form of artificial intelligence enters the scene.

In debates about the relation between human and artificial intelligence, dividual capacity often seems to get lost due to the limitation of the discussion to individual minds. Whether it be the chess computer defeating the grandmaster or the so-called "singularity" of the point at which artificial intelligence exceeds human intelligence, it is mostly about individual or, at best, networked superintelligences, which seem to have nothing to do with dividual flows. Below this struggle of individuals, however, beneath the opposition of human and artificial intelligence and all around it, lies a land in which technical apparatuses and human intellects brace and embrace.

The struggle here is not between an impersonal networked superintelligence and the individual human intellect, but for an intellect that traverses and braces transversely, an intellect that no longer lays claim to being public or universal. It is not an intellect enclosed in the machine or in one spirit, but one possessed by, traversed by and traversing many spirits. Only as transversal intellect – only when connected and appended to many knowledge machines as well as social machines – do ruminations and machinations fire up and start their dividual thinking. Connecting and appending require more than simply having access to knowledge banks and databases in libraries and digital archives; they require engagement in living, social, sensual, and sometimes nonsensical exchanges and experiences within the technecological surround. In this respect, the organs of the transversal intellect are neither a model nor a vanguard of the social machines, nor are they merely writing apparatuses analyzing and evaluating after the fact. It is in the joining of social movements and text machines that the orgic organs of the transversal intellect emerge and unfold.

The transversal intellect is the machine of dividual thinking; more than a networking of individual brains, it runs stream-like through the middle of technical apparatuses and social machines. It engages not in "Querdenken" as querulous and renitent-identitarian thought, but in a queer, transversal, dividual thinking which remains unruly in all its co-formity, consistently turbulent and troublesome.

13

Of Queer Bracing of Time and of Lurking for What Was

As celestial bodies form constellations in the sky, so do times brace. The subjects of this bracing are not static, but asymmetrical, capricious, erratic. Sometimes those long past call their queer siblings in the now; sometimes those of today begin to seek proximities in the distance of earlier times. Their correspondences can go in all directions, but not as a straight line forward: farnearness is not in the future.

There are different practices of reading constellations, whether the astrologer's interpretation of the heavens, the financial trader's reading of an algorithmic constellation, or the longtermist's techno-utopian vision of the stars no longer for terrestrial purposes but for their project of colonizing space. All this is quite spaced out, and not necessarily in a good sense. It is problematic to deduce from it the destinies of the interpreted constellations, and even more problematic to deform our present on the basis of such deductions.

Those who control and conjoin time also want to conjoin the future: "Our future," "a better future for our children," Future of Life and Future of Humanity Institutes, Churches of Artificial Intelligence, longtermist utopias and short-term futures, transhumanist immortality. Predicting the future, proclaiming it, enjoining it, is impossible, even for the most intelligent of artificial intelligences; but predicting the future is not what this is about either. This haunted hunt for the future wants to live down the present. At stake is not so much the colonization of the future, but access to the present as now-time. Through combinations of calculation and prediction, the future, the nearest and the farthest, is determined by counting everything uncountable, making everything immeasurable measurable, adjusting every difference and dissimilarity, and then – or, better, at the same time – adjusting our present to this now determined future. AI and its human helpers simulate *creatio ex nihilo*, and artificial intelligence thus places itself in the succession of artistic invention and divine creation. What is at stake in this case, however, with creation out of nothing, is neither divine nor artistic, and it is by no means a mystical-materialistic becoming nothing: it is the erasure of the past and the emptying of the present. This empty present of the traders and longtermists projects a straight line into the future, in order to dominate the extended present of now-time and erase its extension and tension, its constellation.

The longtermist program dreams of the abstract rescue of humanity from man-made catastrophes, but this works only when the here and now has become a blank slate, when the construction of this blank slate erases the exuberant, chaotic, orgic multiplicity, the subsistential sociality of the extended present. It requires a clipping of the dividual lines in the social space, but also in the depth of a fragile past. The blank slate of a soothsaid present with its risk assessments, predictions, and preventions crushes the geological-social extension of now-time and the leaps from present becoming into the past and back. Enjoining the future seeks to tame that dangerously unruly expanded present; in machinically determining the future it seeks to command our present's obedience. Determining the *Nu*, calculating the eventfulness of insurrection, identifying queer ungovernability – this is the preventive counter-insurgency of machinic capitalism.

Better humming *no future!*, funked-out, post-punk power, dividual monsters, anti-utopian dissemblages, relying less on the clairvoyance of far-sighted seer-traders than on listening to the vague resonances of insurrection and reading dis-sonant echoes, right here, right now. Like a child who, held horizontally, is not interested in the breaking of the waves out there, but only in their foaming extensions below, looking straight down at the foam of the waves, at the spray carried by the extensions of the past wave, and the spatial multiplicity around them. Not looking out to the sea, to the rising and falling waves, and wonder-ing whether there might be a tsunami coming. Seeing the signs, reading the lines, the whirls down there and now, but without transcendent explanation, without overcoding interpretation, without anticipation or appropriation of the future, which in truth wants to appropriate the present time.

Instead of rethinking the future and falling for the visions of seers and traders and longterm-ists, we prefer to obtain information about the relationship between the present becoming and the past. Our present is not a blank slate, not a point between perfect and future tense, but an extended present. Its becoming reaches out in fragile relationship with the splinters of a past not of the victors, but of a minor, battered, bruised past of the oppressed. Not a waste of desire for a better future, but rather an appointment between the times, a mystical-messianic-materialistic dividualization of present becoming and return. It expands silently, a dilation of the present, or it bursts, not in order to rejoin the things, not to correct the tones or to autotune, but to leave the voices untuned, undirected, in detuning and bracing. Unsettled ghosts make themselves heard in the sky and down here; in the now gapes the queer time of condividual multiplicity.

Queer, like the German *quer*, beyond its contemporary genealogies since the early twentieth century, comes from the Middle High German *twër* and the verb *twërn*, "to turn, turn around, stir, mix," which in turn is related to the Latin *vertere*, similarly "to turn, turn around." *Vertere*, as in trans-versality, sheds light on the shimmering continuum of meaning of queer, always starting from unruly sexual orientation, non-binarity, and uncountable genders, but overflowing into the radically anti-identitarian philosophy of transversality. Such a philosophy takes intersectionality as its basis – the entanglement, multiple axes and many dimensions of oppression and subjugation – and at the same time goes beyond it: as a theory of bundling and transversally bracing non-normalized unruly usages, minoritarian struggles, and windy kin.

In queer time it is not only the paternal enjoining of space and time, authoritarian determination and the rule of the norm that implode, but also machinic joining. Queer time escapes not only the patriarchal, heteronormative, authoritarian injunction from above, but also the machinic disposability and subservience that today approaches us from all sides, even from a fully disposable self. In the insistent experiment with unruly dividual usages, this self disjoins, rebelling above all against a jointed time. In a queer instant, time disjoins, polyphonic and out of tune, jumping off its hinges and busting the violently straight line of time. The here and now is then not simply a point between past and future, but unjointed and unruly time, the time of insurrection, a disfigured, burst, exposed present. And it is at the same time a stilled time, the extended-sustaining present, which resists being enjoined between past and future.

What strokes us in a *Nu*, what roves around us in an instant, are windy songs from the sessions and struggles of the past, often blown away by molar memory and historiography. Exuberant, they lurk for the forces that will let them out, let them go, set them free. They lurk, as we lurk, and we prick up our ears. Only in a *Nu* does the wending wind sing, only down here does the bracing of time happen.

Improvising in subjunctures, we react to our surroundings. The soprano saxophone plays a theme, the drums suggest a rhythmic phrasing, other instruments join in. So far, so reactive. But there is also an improvisation that lies in wait. An improvisation that waits for the return of dividual experience. The subjuncture not only disposes of spontaneous presence, of what is there and what is around. It also braces what is becoming with what has been. To be eager for what was means to hold the tension, to remain in the tension until, in an instant, the return of dividual experience occurs.

Revolutionary im/patience, waiting for what was. In sessions and struggles, in rehearsal rooms and strikes, we wait for the moment of return. Becoming eager for what was: even when the music is over, music continues to play somewhere. And both social and musical improvisation, and even more so both together, lie in wait for every little everyday epiphany of the social, for the sociopoetic event, the moment when the music starts playing again.

14

Of Non/Conforming Masses

The mass is frequently demonized as a rabble, a regressive mass, an outlet for the suppression of drives that reproduces leaders, determined by the counterrevolutionary instincts of either the petty bourgeoisie or the lumpenproletariat, easy prey for a wide variety of fascisms, a baiting mass whose phobia of contact seems paradoxically suspended by its multiple contacts. This paradox of the reactionary baiting mass points beyond itself, to a simultaneity of density and dispersion, proximity and distance, contact and detachment, which realigns with the technopolitical developments of recent decades, ambivalently, but also with emancipatory potential. The internet and social media have produced masses that initially appear completely dispersed. But it is in the rage joints of corporate social media that new forms of condensation appear, redistributing the relations of docility and noncompliance, conformism and nonconformity. In phenomena such as the subservient renitence of "rage citizens" and querulous "contrarian thinkers," a disobedience emerges that fits all too well into the rage joint. Renitence is paired with resilience, not as a capacity for resistance, but on the contrary as a capacity for adaptation, for enduring more and more, complying more and more, bearing more and more, with all the rage and all the hatred. Here, obstinate affect fits perfectly into the joints, nonconformity into preformed and further forming forms.

In the realms of individual distinction there might be a fine line, or even a clear binarity, between the good schizo or queer killjoy on the one side and the bad contrarian or querulous rage citizen on the other. But individual characters can be only morally assessed and denounced; there is no possibility of sociopolitical differentiation on this individual level. Only in the transgression from the individual to dividuality – to the subjuncture, the transversal, and co-formity

– can distinctions be made between different modes of relationality, different usages, different mass forms.

On this plane of dividual relationality, a response to the paradoxical phenomenon of renitence and conformism can be conceptualized in terms of a non/conforming mass that is as much conforming as it is nonconformist. Against the grain of the common meaning of "conformity" and "conformism" as moral designations of adaptation and adaptability, conformity here consists in the emphasis on a form that connotes machinic exchange as co-formity, and at the same time promotes a joining that remains unruly. Conforming here does not imply the follower complying with and in the one form and unity. According to scholastic doctrine, co-formity is precisely not uniformity, identity, and docility in the face of this one form. Never homogeneous, co-formity can only be experienced as a becoming similar. Co-forming is that which shares a becoming similar, an approach, a coming close, an approximation, all this without sameness. Closeness in distance, farnear neighborhood, windy kin. Co-forming means sharing similar forms, not owning or appropriating them; not numerical similarity, enumerable territory, or numerable property, but a machinic exchange of forms, multiformity as form-mutation.

In this sense, co-formity does not turn the mass into a unanimous, uniform or authoritatively guided and conformist body, but remains a figure of mutual bracing. The mass is not just dense, and thus prone to baiting, it is near and far at the same time, not unified, but a continuously co-formed and conforming mass. Co-formity here involves no formalism; it does not posit the forms against the contents; rather, it is a bracing of forms of expression and modes of enunciation, forms of organization and modes of existence, in multiplicity.

Nonconformity, on the other hand, describes the mass as an elusive assemblage, against any government as state power or as self-government, nonconforming in its rejection of standardization and normalization. Nonconforming, then, both outwardly and inwardly. The components that compose the mass do not have to adapt, align, or join outwardly nor inwardly in order to suffice themselves, to resemble themselves, to become like each other. Mass is understood here as both dense and dispersed at the same time, as near and yet far. Near not in the sense of touching, body to body, or even forming an organic body, but, if a body at all, then an organless, orgic body, whose un-organs are just as unruly as their dis/sembled dissemblage.

In this complexity, the mass is a non/conforming mass, conforming and nonconformist at the same time. An un/dense, loosely stagnating, nimbly stable, dividually dispersed mass, whether in the public space of the streets and urban squares, in the virtual space of the internet and social media, or in hybrid mixed spaces; a mass in assembling and dissembling, at once unruly and co-forming, but not individualized and enjoined into the rage joint.

In contrast to these two components of the non/conforming mass – conformity as co-formity and nonconformity as unconformable ungovernability – the joining of "rage citizens" and querulous "contrarian thinkers" is evidently its inverse form. While their nonconformism fits into the joints of rage, they paradoxically lack co-formity. They become baiting masses, in turn generating baiting individuals en masse. Without any co-formity, they remain in the machinic-capitalist constitution, caught between sharpened possessive individualism and deindividuation. Only through the double condition of non/conforming usage can there be any emancipatory turn away from the joining of individuals in the specific dense mass of a rage joint. Only with dividual usages, machinic relations and co-forming transmutations can nonconformity and co-formity imply each other as dissemblage.

15

Of Condividual Revolution

In the nineteenth and early twentieth centuries, a particular type of revolution prevailed as a grand and homogenizing paradigm: the linear-molar revolution, which operates with blocs, subjects, and strategies, and arranges the various components of the revolutionary machine on a straight timeline. A period of resistance is followed by the climax of a more or less violent insurrection, which, as it were, naturally culminates in the takeover of the state apparatus. The many currents of revolution, their minor voices and minor histories, were and are straightened out in this paradigm and limited to a fixation on a single lure, the state and its takeover. The multiplicity of revolutionary machines is reduced to the event of insurrection, their spatial and temporal asymmetries and asynchronies forfeit their manifold dimensions, and socially situated subjunctures are lost in the canonized parameters of classical theories of revolution. Takeover of the state apparatus, transfer of state power from one ruling class to another, limitation of the revolution to the exchange of personnel and content – this is how revolution works, by putting the right people and contents in place of the wrong people and contents. If one understands the state apparatus as something neutral, which one only has to operate well and democratically, then it does not have to be reshaped either – the institutional form, the form of the state itself, remains intact.

If this logic takes precedence over social cooperation, it undermines the social machines in the long run. And even in a successful revolution, which pays as much attention to social and economic aspects as to political ones in the narrower sense, the problems of structuralization, state apparatization, and institutional closure remain. So many revolutions, especially the "great" ones like the French and the Russian, could do little to counter this terror of structuralization. Parties of institutionalized revolution, apparatuses occluding the revolution in institutions, state apparatuses as torture benches for social machines: with the decline of the institutionalized and organized working class, with the decay and collapse of state socialism (also in its anti-colonial forms), and with the erosion of democratic socialism and social democracy, it can at least be said even more clearly how revolution does not work.

The music of condividual revolution plays on a completely different terrain: as machinic-social assembling and dissembling, reinvention and recomposition of sociality beyond the state and before the state, without any idea of just taking over the state, but focused rather on its radical transformation. At the same time, accusations that social machines disregard the political, the institutional, the necessity of organizing in general, persist as stubborn misunderstandings, confusing the critique of the state form with naive anarchic ideas. Condividual revolution does not treat the form of the state apparatuses, any more than their contents, as neutral, but as necessarily changeable. It does not universalize questions of organization, but experiments with them in a situated way. This implies, first of all, that the question of organizing should not only focus on the (national) state, the molar dimension of the revolution, but should be thought as dividually as possible, in the joints of situated instituent practices and translocal-transversal machines.

In the 2010s, the strongest genealogical line of this non-state-fixated, instituent revolution appeared first in the occupation movements in the Mediterranean region, spread as the "Arab Spring" and in Spain as 15M, and extended in later offshoots, both smaller and more massive, known mainly as the translocal Occupy movement. The occupations themselves were undoubtedly events of condividual revolution, and in Spain in subsequent years they even developed into serious attempts to transform democratic institutions. With all its influences from the Mediterranean, but also from Latin America, the *municipalismos* movement that followed the occupations intervened less in the state as a nation-state than in the local and translocal politics of the municipalities, enabling radical changes in political content there with its non-representationist perspective. The relation of the municipalist movement to the municipalities was not a subject/object relation, like that of a revolutionary subject seizing possession of its object of desire. Instead of simply taking over the municipality as a super-temporal container whose contents get switched out, the movement also tried to change the institutional form itself. It focused on social issues like the question of debt, the re-municipalization of public services, gentrification and touristification, and the guarantee of social rights in relation to housing and education. When in 2015 the movement enjoyed unexpected electoral success, very diverse components took municipal office for one term in A Coruña, Madrid, Zaragoza, Cádiz and several other cities, and in Barcelona even for two terms (until 2023).

Although the Spanish *municipalismos* were not successful in forcing long-term transformations, they assembled a great deal of radical-reformist experience in a way that had not been possible in Europe for a long time. Their condividual revolution should not be thought of as transcendent, but rather as an immanent transition. The idea of a revolution's transcendence is always problematic both spatially (as a strictly defined anti-capitalist territory, functioning alongside but outside of capitalism) and temporally (as a future socialist paradise, communist utopia, or anti-clerical heaven). The revolution arises precisely on the field of immanence that it shares with capitalist forms. Today, both the modes of production and the technopolitical conditions are designed for dispersion and distribution – but these are also the dividual lines of condividual revolution. Beyond molar organizational narratives of revolutionary history, beyond the historiography that structuralizes it, immanent revolutionary practice consists precisely in drawing dividual lines, in fanning transversal machines that brace the distance. Breaking with linear narratives of revolution, transition also takes on a different meaning to that of a planned transition from capitalism to communism. In this sense, it has always already begun, as an ongoing experiment in new usages, as a chain of instituent practices that has no end point. In the middle of a field of immanence that encompasses both machinic capitalism and condividual revolution, transition itself becomes the terrain, the time and space of communism or, better, of condivision.

Condivision always means both division and sharing, separation and co-formity, dividuality and joining. It is a non-communitarian, non-unifying, non-reductive way of composition. Condividual revolution is a revolution that cannot be enclosed in community and does not conform to the logic of debt; it is a revolution of sharing, exuberant and anti-consumerist, a revolution of dividual lines, unruly bonds, and dispersed bracings. Condividual revolution is a revolution of usages, of forms of use and forms of life, of radical transmutations and technecologies in everyday life and convivialities. Condividual revolution is an affirmation of the manifold, a revolutionary machine intensifying and bracing the distant. Quite differently from the classical timeline for revolution – first resistance, then revolt, then the construction of a new society – this revolutionary machine continuously traverses its three tangling and overlapping components: resistance as primary; post-national and translocal insurrection; constituent power as an uncompleted and incompletable process.

Condividual revolution needs the manifold simultaneity of speeds, slownesses, standstill, and acceleration; not one after the other, but at the same time, alternately, traversing each other. Insurrectional rupture and the duration of resistance and constituent power do not emerge one

after the other, but as appositive and overlapping qualities of the revolutionary machine.
The temporalities of condividual revolution
are complementary: revolutionary patience
needs revolutionary impatience, in simultaneous untimeliness. The time of insurrection, the
blasting now-time of dividual uprising, comes
from duration, from multiplicity in time; only
with this do turbid now-time and the scattered
multiplicity of disjointures condense into a non/
conforming assembly.

Revolutionary duration is the plane of constituent power and subsistential territories. The lines
of condividual revolution traverse the usages, the
modes of conduct, the pores of a resistant everyday life, transforming the molecules of sociality
in a revolutionary traversal of things, instead of
the wholeness, oneness, and universality of the
molar revolution. The social-machinic subjuncture will always have been there, below the radar
of the apparatuses. Our task is to take care of
this subjoining sociality, to extend it and carry
it into the existing state apparatuses in order to
transform them.

Condividual revolution ultimately also entails
the permanent decolonization of machinic

capitalism. In the middle of the immanence field of its coloniality, the logic of dispersion, accumulation, and dividual traversal can be inverted: farnear distribution instead of the spread of derivatives and big data; bracing and assembly instead of the accumulation of capital; dividual lines of anti-capitalist praxis, in caring company, poor possession, and occupation. And in the same middle other maps emerge, different from those of mapping platforms and navigation tools; not copies or digital doubles of the world, not enveloping matrices that overlay everything. Then on the old maps there suddenly appear the extinguished, scraped, erased territories; then also new cartographies reorder the plane of immanence. Drawing its dividual lines, condividual revolution decolonizes machinic capitalism, on the edges, in ephemeras, on occasion, on- and off-line.

16

Of Dissemblage

As machinic capitalism increasingly closes in on authoritarian techno-regimes and fascistoid forms of government, the question of what storming the machines might look like in this current setting seems ever more urgent. Far from being limited to its insurrectionist manifestation, machine storming is involved in all three overlapping components of the revolutionary machine. In the context of twenty-first-century machinic capitalism, it implies different objects than in the Luddite forms of struggle two centuries ago. But it might today still encompass anti-capitalist practices of intervention in the forms of exploitation and precarization of labor in the scattered sites that have taken over the function of the factory. In this genealogy, and in the context of recent ecological movements, machine storming still also includes concrete attacks on plants, infrastructures, apparatuses, and corporations that contribute to ecological catastrophes.

Even so, the storm today must necessarily also be directed against us, against our selves, against the machines in which we are cogs. Again, this is not a moralistic-individualist call for individual lifestyle changes or for anti-technological strategies demanding the destruction of our contemporary digital tools; it is rather a call for social struggles that give rise to dividual usages in the midst of the storm. More-than-human, more-than-individual, these usages start from the middle of everyday lives in subsistential territories, inventing new machinic exchanges, new monstrous forms of relating and organizing. And in this sense, they are also streams and storms and struggles against all forms of identitarian domination. These struggles can only be waged if their resistance is not purely actionist, their insurrection is not insurrectionist, and their constituent power does not degenerate into constituted power (as happens when prohibitions, codes of conduct, professional moderations, or moral principles are imposed upon assemblies and movements).

Insurrection that is not insurrectionist – that does not glorify the one big masculinist event – multiplies the *Nu* as an ongoing chain of extended presents, braced in farnearness and condensed in non/conforming masses. Resistance that is not solely actionist is not content with the spectacular, mediatized performance, but anchors itself in everyday life, in subjunctures and subsistential territories. Constituent power, which is not supposed to rigidify into an institution or a structuralized constituted power, invents and experiments with instituent practices, assemblies, and constituent processes. Insurrection, resistance, and constituent power: these three components of the revolutionary machine require – precisely in machinic capitalism with its joining mechanisms – the disjoining capacity of something that is monstrous, hulking, warping, bulging, garbled; something that can collapse and break apart at any time, that falls apart in letting itself fall, that dissembles while assembling; something that therefore, if it joins at all, never joins exactly, never joins perfectly, never joins completely: a dissemblage.

The dissemblage is an assemblage insofar as it is composed of different lines, parts of machines, things, living beings, spirits, and ghosts. Composition always in a double sense: as being joined and process of joining, as component and process of composition. Never simply connecting existing parts or points, but always lines that bundle and join together. Thus, the dissemblage is not the opposite or negation of an assemblage; it is itself an assemblage, but always before the assemblage, unwilling to be assembled in that way. Undirected, never aligned, never right, never straight: unruly unjoinedness, before all joining, beside and under and all around it.

Dis/sembling is dissociation, but only insofar as it does not refer to a simplified notion of cleavage that starts from the one and splits it into two parts. What constitutes the dissemblage is the drawing of dividual lines, being drawn by those lines, ongoing division and separation, an assembling form of division, division that is at the same time sharing, division that is primary, an association still in dissembling. In the dissemblage, the parts of the assemblage assemble precisely to the extent that they are different, divided, divisible, dispersed, disconnected, separated, and allowed to remain separated. ⌐

The dissemblage is not machinically disposable. It is disposable differently, in another way, for other assemblages, in other temporalities. It is always disposable for what and where it wants to be disposable. Always being free, always being disposable. Under conditions of highest precarity: making time, taking time, stealing time for the unruly things, for the queer struggles, for the windy kin. Nobody calls their meeting, nobody starts it, nobody governs it. Instead of joining disobedience into the joints of rage, the dissemblage remains unruly in the middle of its co-formity.

The dissemblage does not comply, it is unconformable, disobedient, unwilling. It does not want to obey, to be made the same, to be one; it does not want to be whole. In this sense, it is disjointure before being enjoined, before the violence by which it is pursued. It doesn't want to be complete, it doesn't want to be perfect, it prefers to remain in the joints out of joint. Its forms form apart and together, conforming and nonconforming. For all its co-formity, it remains out of form. Ungovernable, monstrous in all its wild softness, below the grand plan and all around it, it is intangible and out of shape, a patchwork of abrupt breaks and loose bands, gaps and provisional seams. Its cacophony is multijoining – there are too many voices, too wild and too minor, to fit them all into one. Always many minor voices fleeing in all directions, many-jointed, falling out of joint and always finding new joints. Nonsense, mischief, asignificance, craziness, senselessness, and the subversion of any search for meaning. Mad, yet not without spirit, rather with so many spirits, possessed by the transversal intellect, traversed by multiplicities of things, a dissembled, unassembled, and unassemblable dissemblage.

17

Of Multiplicity

Over the last twenty years, there has been a growing number of voices claiming that anti-identitarian, non-binary, queer, post-migrant, transversal, and multitudinarian positions have gone too far both discursively and in their practices. As "postmodernists" they would be virtually responsible for the catastrophic capitalist transformations of the past five decades. They should at least take a step back in favor of tactical compromises, left populisms, strategic subordination to political leaders, and reformist approaches focused on taking over or defending existing structures and institutions.

On the contrary! The conceptual and political experiments in multiplicity never went far enough – there was still too little machination, too little condivision, too little transversality, too little multiplicity. A materialist-immanent philosophy of multiplicity means not depriving the practices and theories of multiplicity of their radicality, but pushing them further in the struggles, over unexpected folds and along even the flattest of surfaces, beyond previous approaches and historical experiences. Multiplicity has not yet been pushed far enough, not thought, not machinated, not made far enough.

Since the ancients, multiplicity has been regularly disdained in very different philosophical approaches, treated with resentment or exclusively considered in its relation to the one. As disordered, structureless, unmanageable, and lacking in determination, it has led a dependent-subordinate existence in the lack and bustle of appearances. In moralizing philosophical discourses, multiplicity is traditionally associated with the false, the evil, and the ugly, with disunity, formlessness, and confusion. Fed by ecclesiastical sources, the one, while always entangled in contradictions and complications even in theology, dominates the ontological scene: the one and the many, the one against the many, the one before the many, the one above the many, the many descending from the one, the many determined by the one, the many composed of units, the many sublated in the one, the many dissolved in the one – always the primacy of the one with its operations of unification, sublation, extinction.

Defecting from this hierarchical relation means thinking multiplicity no longer as a mere derivation, a descent from the primordial one or a transition to the one, nor in any new relation to the one; it means rather thinking multiplicity radically without unity, irreducible and innumerable, the many without the one. Not only against the one, but going beyond it, through it, under it, and around it, leaping in all directions, into the folds of time. Making multiplicity, and at the same time lurking for past multiplicity, if and when it returns; listening to the stories, the melodies and rhythms of multiplicity in queer bracing, even if they sound small and low, immature and confused, hummed by many minor voices.

Machinic capitalism seeks to modulate multiplicity and make it disposable in processes of accumulation even when it is non-numerical, and without having to resort directly to the old methods of identifying, counting, and measuring. The modulation of productivity functions here through machinic disposability and subservience, dispersion and voluntary self-control. Even the unidentifiable and uncountable may be accumulated without clear processes of striating, overcoding, and appropriation. All that is disposable joins to the joints, and what is not yet jointed is made disposable without joining.

Yet, this does not mean we need to fall back on ideas of disobedience and revolution, in which for their part the many are homogenized and totalized. For the many, even in their negative appearance as modulated and joined multiplicity, which is nothing else than diversity, there is no way "back" into an imagined one, into unity and oneness, but only the unfolding and traversing of the many in their immanent middle. On exactly this field of immanence, every obedient-joined diversity can mutate into an unruly multiplicity, an unjoined, ungovernable, condividual multiplicity – unfolding and further folding the many folds, entangling the windy kin, multiplying and complicating its unmunt.

Down here, here and now, in the turbu-
lences of condivision, hatred and resentment
can turn into affirmation and apposition, baiting masses can mutate into multiplicities, those
isolated and lonely in disobedience can become
dissembling assemblages, self-pitying trolls can
dissolve into technecologies, baiting media into
transversal machines. Down here, in subsistential territories and expanded presents, we can,
beyond the obedience of renitent-identitarian
contrarian thought, try out a queer, transversal, dividual thinking that remains unruly from
its middle and in all its co-formity. A transversal and queer thinking, always starting out
from unruly sexual orientation, non-binarity,
and uncountable genders, but escalating into a
radically anti-identitarian philosophy of transversality. Down here in the middle, the streams
of desire redirect us to assemblies of farnearness and nonconformist co-formity, to other
usages, other forms of living together, as the
machinic production of desire brings forth new
ways of "self"-organization that disjoin every
self-governed self, subjoin isolation, and shift
asymmetries in the orgic organization of a revolutionary multiplicity.

There is no empty land, no empty map, only bulging nothingness and murky multiplicity. Staying down here, in the turbid, in the queer, in transitions and transverses, never arriving in identity, not even new identity, but staying scattered, multijoining and manifold in transversal machines. Trans-thing, sub- and supernatural thing, in seas, in nothingness, in the subjunctures, scattering and expanding outside the order and under the grand plan, without any idea of the one. Beyond its mere invocation, making multiplicity in dividual thought, transversal intellect, and condividual revolution.

Our struggles for multiplicity will always be manifold struggles, struggles of non/conforming masses, unruly and co-forming, struggles that not only endure the double division but keep on pushing it forward, divided and sharing at the same time, manifold-co-forming, condividual. And in the manifold folding, the most distant can come into close proximity, keeping the joints em/braced. Dissemblage, which is not to be made disposable in such a way, not to be taken into service in such a way, not to be put into value in such a way, and if it is, nevertheless, in its unconformable co-formity resists accumulation, and if it does not, instills, inserts, and feeds its blemishes, pimples, bumps, humps, outflows, scales, spikes, thorns, horns, barbs, bugs, and glitches into the streams of accumulation, so that the algorithms collapse and multiplicity multiplies.